CELTIC
MELTDOWN

Cearbhall Ó Dálaigh from Kerry emigrated to America in 1970 and returned to Ireland in 1978. He invested in and worked in the tourism and fishing industries and sold those interests in 1990. He then worked with the EU-TACIS programme in the early 1990s. From the mid-1990s to 2007 he was a subcontractor in the Irish construction industry. His interests lie in economics and Irish politics.

http://celticmeltdown.webs.com

CELTIC MELTDOWN

Why Ireland is Broke and How We Can Fix It

CEARBHALL Ó DÁLAIGH

The Collins Press

FIRST PUBLISHED IN 2009 BY
The Collins Press
West Link Park
Doughcloyne
Wilton
Cork

British Library Cataloguing in Publication Data

O Dalaigh, Cearbhall.
  Celtic meltdown : why Ireland is broke and how we can fix it.
  1. Fiscal policy—Ireland. 2. Ireland—Economic conditions—
  21st century.
  I. Title
  336.3'09417-dc22

ISBN-13: 9781848890121

Typesetting by Carrigboy Typesetting Services
Typeset in Berkeley
Printed in Great Britain by J F Print Ltd

'When bad men combine, the good must associate; else they will fall one by one, an unpitied sacrifice in a contemptible struggle'

Edmund Burke

CONTENTS

Introduction

THE WAY FORWARD

*'It is hard to fail, but it is much worse
never to have tried to succeed.'*
Theodore Roosevelt

C an we fix this? Yes, we can. I believe that with a series of new approaches in banking, business, government and the public service, we can fix Ireland Inc. This book maps out new possible strategic paths forward for the Irish economy, ones which should also enhance social cohesion through greater transparency and accountability in the offices and mechanisms of public and commercial life.

This book is driven by optimism, and by a desire to see Ireland get back on its feet. However, we cannot go forward without first looking back at some of our recent mistakes, otherwise we would run the risk of repeating them. So *Celtic Meltdown* also reflects upon and analyses the arrival of the

Celtic Tiger years, retraces key moments in its rise and the deep flaws which have hastened its crushing demise.

This book looks at the causes behind Ireland's present crisis, and then suggests a series of solutions. Some of these proposals are near-term, relating to mechanisms to better manage Irish banking, politics and business life. Other proposals relate to longer-term planning for employment and wealth generation, notably in the key areas of energy and green technologies. Great business opportunities exist in the generation of renewable energies.

The Irish people have some very serious decisions to make. We need a new direction. We will not achieve that without new ideas and a willingness to change. We will not rebuild our shattered economy with mantras alone. When Barack Obama says 'yes we can' it carries fervent echoes of Martin Luther King. In Brian Cowen's mouth, such a mantra has a hollow ring, emanating from the undeserved leader of an incompetent government presiding over a corrupt banking sector and a system of crony capitalism.

America has had to endure flooding of biblical proportions, terrorism and deep social decay; it has had to bottom out before it could finally take its first tentative steps towards a better future. We too must go through some pain and serious self-analysis to avoid repeating the mistakes of the past, before we can begin to create a better and more secure path forward. We must stop looking for short cuts and economic miracles. Instead, we must be brave enough to oust the corrupt and write some new rules.

So where to begin? Let's start with the present.

Ireland needs to focus on becoming a productive economy once again. This time, however, we need more solid foundations, with none of the previous manic, speculative activities led by the financial sector and property speculators.

In the immediate term, where would Ireland find the money to stimulate the economy? The country currently has about €300 billion in deposits and this money is looking for a safe home.

Ireland could raise a national recovery bond, which could be structured in such a way that it would attract these funds and put them to productive use in rebuilding the economy. This is the only way Ireland will break out of the current decline. Any other course of action, such as raising taxes, will simply turn the recession into a depression. What worked yesterday will certainly not work tomorrow, because our banks are busted, the economy is busted and we need to consign all previous economic policies to the dustbin of history.

Giving banks more taxpayers' money simply to keep them on life support is reckless in the extreme. The government speaks about bank bailouts, but they are not bailing out anything, because insolvency, and not liquidity, is the real cause of the Irish banking crisis.

The major Irish banks are dead. High net worth individuals will give them a wide berth after the wealth destruction they have caused over the past two years. You really do need to have your head examined if you're willing to trust these banks with your money after what they have done. That is why the banks are now out of capital and nobody wants to own their shares. That is why these same banks now see the Irish taxpayers as the very last source of capital available for them to plunder.

The excesses of the past five years have left Ireland nearly bankrupt. Our future as a sovereign nation now depends upon our ability to take control of events and properly govern our economy, to control public sector spending and sort out the banking sector. If confidence in the system is to be restored, these two tasks need to occur simultaneously, because sorting out these issues will be the foundation of future success.

Everybody will have different ideas on how this can be achieved and many are probably valid. Unorthodox ideas, like those contained in this book, must be given an airing.

We must also be willing to accept making a few mistakes, because if we learn from our mistakes then we can turn failure to our advantage. A fear of failure is a terribly inhibiting trait, because if we fear failure we will never try anything new.

Let us look at a few examples of how one maverick's unconventional ideas can benefit the whole herd. Back in the 1990s, a young Irish telecoms entrepreneur called Denis O'Brien tackled the might of the then state telephone monopoly, Telecom Éireann. O'Brien triumphed and within ten years became a multimillionaire. At the time, everybody told him he was crazy and destined for failure, but he soldiered on and triumphed against mighty odds, eventually selling his business to British Telecom for €2 billion.

Tony Ryan and Michael O'Leary did the same with Ryanair. Everybody told them they could never succeed against the mighty state monopoly airline, Aer Lingus. But they did succeed and Ryanair is now one of the largest and most successful airlines in Europe, far bigger and hugely more profitable than Aer Lingus.

Throughout Ireland there are many more examples, just like these, of people who have achieved great success against staggering odds. This entrepreneurial spirit is alive and well in Ireland and must now be harnessed to help the nation out of its current crisis.

There are, however, some key issues to be tackled if we are to have the scope and freedom to put Ireland on a prosperous path to the future. This time our government needs to do better forward planning than they have done over the past ten years and commit to making decisions which are in the long-term best interest of the country.

So, with the greater goal of Ireland's ultimate recovery in mind, let us now start to reflect upon how Ireland has come to find itself in its present sorry state. During the course of this book, we will tease out the threads of solutions to each of Ireland's major social and economic problems, then gather these concepts into a properly formulated road map for change in the closing chapters.

Chapter 1

WHEN THE CHICKENS CAME HOME TO ROOST

Tuesday 30 September 2008 was the day that the Irish state bank guarantee heralded the death knell of the Celtic Tiger. Ireland's moment of truth had finally arrived.

A few Irish economic prophets had been warning of the imminent arrival of this day for about two years. These same economists had been pilloried and ostracised by the politicians, bankers and businessmen as 'prophets of doom' and accused of acting unpatriotically, but the inevitable had happened and Ireland's chickens had finally come home to roost.

Tax revenues collapsed, creating a disaster for the government finances. Unemployment was soaring. Some 9,000 people per week lost their jobs in January 2009 alone. Irish banks had been exposed as having engaged in fraud on a massive scale, with illegal share support schemes and billions being improperly transferred between banks, and most of those banks would have gone into bankruptcy if the government had not made the Irish people accept liability for the astronomical debts and losses these bankers had run up.

There was no mistaking the truth, the Celtic Tiger was well and truly dead and the party was definitely over.

But, as Tommy Tiernan would say, *'or was it?'* In January 2009, there were still quite a few delusional souls around who were in total denial as to the enormity of the economic situation facing the country. The banks were still not admitting they had bankrupted the nation. The property sections of newspapers still carried advertisements (although far fewer) offering bungalows in the middle of nowhere for half a million.

We had a Taoiseach, who in the preceding years had been in control of the economy as Minister for Finance, bellowing in the Dáil, 'I'll run the country the way I see fit'. Quite an extraordinary outburst coming from a man who had previously informed the house about the need for a 'more uplifting' quality of debate that would change the 'adversarial nature' of a 'political narrative' that damages 'the dignity of the house'.

Also, there were still a few property developers around who were trying to get planning permission for grandiose schemes that had not even the faintest hope of ever being financed or built. The public sector unions were in total denial regarding the true state of affairs of Ireland's economy.

It was a very painful and scary time of readjustment for all those people who previously thought they could walk on water.

The politicians had to adjust to the idea that tax revenues were going down sharply and would do so for many years to come. The government folly of not saving any money during the good times was now becoming painfully obvious and they were being forced to accept that if they did not take this into account and quickly adjust spending, the international markets, on whom Ireland now depended for borrowings, would force them to do so.

Ireland was faced with the certainly of losing its AAA credit rating as the deterioration in public finances was becoming more evident with each passing day, and while it was unrealistic to talk of the country defaulting on its debts, there was no doubt that Ireland was facing into a decade of retrenchment, just as it did in the 1980s, as it struggled to get borrowing and government debt back under control.

At the beginning of 2009, the government faced two major problems. One was the increase in the national debt brought about by the government taking responsibility for the banks' enormous debts of about (nobody seemed to know the true figure, not even the bankers) €500 billion. The other problem was the collapse in tax revenue. Income tax, corporation tax, VAT, PAYE and PRSI were all down. The government had to move fast if events were to be prevented from spiralling out of control.

But, unfortunately, in the first months of 2009 the government was showing no signs that it had any sort of realistic and coherent plan for dealing with the myriad problems unfolding each day.

The Taoiseach was a lawyer from Offaly, the Deputy Taoiseach was a social worker from Donegal and the Minister for Finance was a Dublin barrister more used to pleading cases in court. All three were members of the Dáil simply because their fathers held their seats before them. Hardly the most qualified group of people to man the ramparts in Ireland's hour of need. They say that in a democracy you get the government you deserve. If that's true, then the Irish people must have done some awfully bad things to deserve this lot.

By the end of February 2009, the government had belatedly sent the Garda Fraud Squad into Anglo Irish Bank, something that should have been done months earlier. But even this late move was probably only prompted as a result of an announcement by the European Central Bank (ECB) that they were about to take a more active regulatory oversight role of Eurozone central banks. One would have expected the government to have also sent the fraud squad into Irish Life & Permanent on the same day, as they were equally complicit in Anglo's shady dealings, but once again the government displayed a failure to act decisively.

Clouds were looming everywhere. The problem for the government was not just the recession, for that had barely begun. The real problem was the soaring unemployment levels, with the consequent twofold hit of increased social welfare payments and the loss of PAYE/PRSI revenue.

The high unemployment levels also led to a decline in consumer spending which was, in turn, followed by a severe drop in tax revenue from the retail and hospitality sectors. There was a large loss of corporation tax across the boards as countless Irish businesses began to go into liquidation. The housing slump knocked a huge hole in the stamp-duty take, and the collapse of the construction sector left a large building materials VAT deficit. The country's economy was in a critical downward vortex and in danger of spinning out of control.

The public sector unions had abandoned the notion of 'social partnership' and were hell-bent on copper-fastening the notion of secure public sector employment, with high levels of pay and pensions, and to hell with the rest of the country.

Meanwhile, the private sector was suffering massive pay cuts and redundancies, with a third of a million unemployed and heading for half a million by year's end.

The increased rise in the level of unemployment would mean further declines in the property market, well into 2010 and beyond. All activity had dried up in the real-estate market and any people who were forced to sell had to do so at prices that were down 50 per cent from their peaks at mid-2007.

In the spring of 2009, the country needed strong and decisive leadership, but Taoiseach Brian Cowen sat in the Dáil with a look of defeat on his face and the Minister of Finance Brian Lenihan seemed to be outmanoeuvred by the banks at every turn. It was hard to be optimistic because even if the government did clamp down on spending, it would take a while for that to have an effect. There are good reasons not to cut public spending in a slump, but the government would have needed savings to avoid doing so and there were no savings. The huge tax proceeds of the boom years had all been spent.

Back in 2004, there could have been a debate as to whether the burden should be borne mainly by cutting spending or by increasing taxation. Now it was clear that it would have to be both. The perilous state of the economy made radical measures inevitable, and the unenviable task for the government was how to sustain broad electoral support for these measures.

The bigger issue dawning on the population at large was that we were getting a taste of the sort of fiscal constraints that would govern political policy for a long time. Because we were now faced with borrowing billions just to meet day-to-day spending and every single euro of those borrowings would have to be paid back.

The Irish economy's plight was partly a result of international recession but also one of structural imbalance. We were not generating enough tax revenue for the level of public spending which had been put in place over the previous five years. Unfortunately, that imbalance, as the private sector contracts dramatically, is destined to grow ever larger.

Demographics are also a problem in this regard, as an ageing population will require more spending on health care and pensions. A falling working population will have to fund those services. So it is a question of paying more tax for the same level of services, and maybe for worse or at least cheaper services.

The outlook for Ireland was very dismal in the spring of 2009. Once again, as in previous generations, young people were voting with their feet by emigrating.

Until the spring of 2009 it had not been necessary to confront this situation, for three main reasons. One was the relative strength of tax revenues. The second was the general strength of the economy, itself a result of excessive private borrowing. The third had been a doubling in the size of the workforce from 1 to 2 million, partly from inward migration and partly because people above retirement age had to remain in the workforce as their pension savings had disappeared.

Leadership style: Obama v. Cowen

January 2009. Barack Obama is looking out of his window. His thoughts drift towards Washington's financial institutions far beyond his gaze, and the bankers who reside there. The newly elected US President has just read a report outlining bonuses for US financial executives, which topped $18 billion during 2008. The report noted that the total was down more than 40 per cent from the previous year.

Over his shoulder, a team of advisers sit at table, their heads turned in the direction of the new leader of the Western World, only occasionally glancing questioningly at one another, like dogs wondering in which direction their master will throw the stick. What will Obama do? What are the legal parameters? Or, in this instance, will leadership be more important than legality? It is a decisive first test.

4 February 2009. Obama stands before the US media, with Treasury Secretary Timothy Geithner by his side. 'For top executives to award themselves these kinds of compensation packages in the midst of this economic crisis is not only in bad taste, it is a bad strategy, and I will not tolerate it as President,' he said.

The president announced a $500,000 yearly limit on compensation for executives of companies receiving emergency federal assistance. He added that any companies that had been bailed out would be required to disclose all benefits provided to their top managers, and that severance packages would be limited.

The decision to bail out the banks was not Obama's. His predecessors had approved a $700-billion rescue package for financial firms, the biggest bailout fund in US history. No doubt Obama would have done likewise, but with the control measures he was now exacting. The President said he wanted to ensure that executives would not be rewarded for failure while being subsidised by US taxpayers. The bankers questioned the legality of these control measures, arguing that they were not in place when the Republican-led Congress approved the bailout. Obama has simply eyeballed them down. There's a new sheriff in town.

Meanwhile, back in Ireland.

29 January 2009. Taoiseach Brian Cowen is delivering a speech to the Irish media. Not for the first time, he reminds us that we should be careful about what we say on the state of the Irish economy. He says we should be more like the Americans in the way that they support their President. He describes people who criticise him and his government as being 'unpatriotic'.

Perhaps there are reasons why Americans find it easier to support Barack Obama than it is for Irish people to support Brian Cowen. The American people are responding to real and instant solutions. In a word, they are responding to leadership. Ireland's handling of its banking crisis has none of that sense of swift justice. Our vague, under-researched crisis management compares very poorly with the US. It also compares very poorly with our EU neighbours.

By December 2008, just like the USA and Ireland, many Eurozone countries had also put in place solutions to help their banks recapitalise. Germany approved a package worth up to €500 billion. In France, the figure was about €350 billion. Spain set aside €100 billion. All, bar Ireland, have imposed restrictions and government vetoes dictating how the banks would operate henceforth. Ireland's government has committed its taxpayers to bank liabilities of €485 billion. This is almost the same amount that Germany has allowed for the restructuring of its entire banking system. But Germany has the largest economy in the EU and fourth largest in the world. In 2006 and 2007, Germany was also the world's largest exporter by value, greater than even the US or China. And the bank bailout figure for Ireland is as large as that of Germany? Something was beginning to really stink.

All truth passes through three stages.

Firstly, it is ridiculed.

Secondly, it is violently opposed.

Thirdly, it is accepted as being self-evident.

In Ireland, truths are something we rarely get to hold as self-evident. Ireland is not America, not at any level.

President Obama and Brian Cowen are both the same age, but they share little else in common. Obama is full of energy, brimming with ideas, surrounded by bright, independent people and has created a clear road map for getting his people out of the enormous difficulties his predecessor George Bush landed them in.

Brian Cowen, on the other hand, appears tired, devoid of ideas, surrounded only by supporters who tell him what a great man he is. He has failed to create a road map for getting his people out of the enormous difficulties into which Brian Cowen himself dropped them during his terms as finance minister and as Taoiseach. He substitutes bombastic bullying for reasoned debate. When he goes overseas he tells the Emperor of Japan that what the Irish and Japanese have in common is a love of sculling pints of porter. Such statements illustrate just how hugely out of touch with reality Cowen really is.

This disconnectedness from reality is best illustrated when one sees what Cowen believes is a fair income for the work he does, in comparison to other world leaders:

Brian Cowen, Irish Taoiseach	€5,990 per week
Barack Obama, US President	€5,300 per week
Angela Merkel, German Chancellor	€4,350 per week

Cowen's style of government also does little to engender voter admiration. When he sought to save €70 million in the 2008 budget, he suggested removing free medical services from one of the most vulnerable sections of society, namely old-age pensioners.

Yet in 2007 to 2008, his government spent €158.5 million on private consultants and spin doctors. In December 2008, he cancelled a vaccination programme which would protect young Irish girls from cervical cancer in order to save €10 million.

The Irish pork industry is worth €385 million per year to the economy, but in December 2008 when the pork processors were out of action for *one week*, they got €180 million compensation from Brian Cowen. It is only pure coincidence, of course, that many of these processors are located around his home towns of Tullamore and Roscrea.

Cowen and his cabinet currently look like rabbits staring into the headlights of an oncoming car that is going to roll right over them. It is as if they don't know what to do, now that none of the yarns spun at huge cost by their outsized PR machine have turned out to be true. Perhaps the greatest of these myths relates to the contribution of 'social partnership' to Ireland's financial well-being over the past ten years. For the past decade, the Irish public have been treated to regular pageants of late-night negotiations between the government and the unions. The dénouement has always been the same: a 'hard won' deal in which the unions agreed to an annual pay increase of 2 per cent or more 'for the good of the nation'.

In reality, the 'social partners' did very well out of these negotiations, consistently beating both inflation and private sector increases. But the biggest winners of all were the politicians themselves, whose already exorbitant salaries are now linked to that of a principal officer in the civil service. Each time the partners gained 6 per cent over twenty-seven months, the politicians gained too, only their 6 per cent was worth far more as it was a percentage of an already grossly over-inflated salary.

Hard-fought negotiations? In reality, social partnership has been a late-night divvying-up of the spoils between the poachers and the gamekeepers. Benchmarking has paid off hugely for the politicians, but this venality has now been carefully airbrushed out of history by the government's PR machine. The Taoiseach and his chums paid themselves more than the US president and his staff, and the Irish public applauded the 'sacrifice' they were making for the nation. Partnership? More like a divine comedy.

Partnership has not been the only ruse of recent years. Much of Ireland's new Celtic Tiger wealth was dangerously dependent on the property market so, like the property-market bubble, a lot of this new private sector wealth was an illusion destined to vanish when the property boom came to a sudden and inglorious end. And as this wealth vanished, the gap between Ireland's public and private sectors widened dramatically.

- In the six years between 2001 and 2006, public sector salaries rose by 59 per cent. The increase in the average industrial wage over the same period was 19 per cent.
- Salaries, and not services, are far and away the major input cost in our public sector, including the Health Service.
- The public sector pay bill now accounts for 38 per cent of total government spending and this percentage is set to rise dramatically in 2009 as tax revenues collapse.
- The public sector pay/pensions bill for 2008 is €18.6 billion and will be over €20 billion in 2009.
- From 2001–2006, public sector pensions increased by 81.3 per cent, from €876 million to €1.5 billion.
- Retired civil servants who sit on job interview panels earn up to €878 per day.

- There are 370,000 people on the public payroll and in the period between 2001 and 2006 public sector worker numbers increased by 38,000.

In December 2008, SIPTU General President Jack O'Connor said, in relation to cuts in public service pay: 'Any savings that would be made by reducing public sector pay would be pennies in terms of the overall problems for the economy'. Given the figures outlined above, these 'pennies' were clearly not being counted and controlled by the Irish government. And why should they? Every time the public service unions gained, the politicians made equal gains via the bench-marking process.

It is very convenient for today's politicians and bankers to lay the blame for the demise of Ireland's economy on 'external forces beyond our control'. Undoubtedly, external forces have had an effect on the ending Ireland's boom, but that is not the full story.

The bulk of our current woes have been of our own creation. There were many political and banking decisions taken here in Ireland, which ensured that our period of boom was going to come to an abrupt end. As we go forward from here and work at rebuilding the Irish economy from the ashes of the boom, it is going to require a lot of hard work and supreme confidence in our own ability to achieve success. This task will be made much more difficult if we fail to identify the mistakes that got us into this situation in the first place. Some of these mistakes must, with Barack Obama-like speed and efficiency, be undone if we are to have any reasonable chance of future success.

The Bankers and their part in our downfall

The bankers, who have been bailed out by the Irish taxpayers, must be compelled to open their books and disclose *exactly* what level of debt they are carrying, both on and off balance sheet.

These debts then need to be properly valued and not carried on the banks' loan books at the fantasy valuations they currently have.

There is a dirty little secret of financial reporting called off-balance-sheet financing (OBSF) and it is directly responsible for the collapse of the Irish banking system.

The term 'off-balance-sheet' debt describes a technique used to shift debt off the company's balance sheet, making the company's fundamentals look far stronger than they actually are. The companies who engage in this practice usually say, 'Not all off-balance-sheet finance is shady and it can be a useful tool that for a variety of legitimate purposes, such as tapping into extra sources of financing and reducing liability risk that could hurt earnings'.

Irish bankers wanted to take on debt while reporting none of it, or only some of it, as liabilities on their balance sheets. They calculated that depriving investors and other financial statement users of this vital information would drive their stock price higher and help create obscene bonuses for bank executives.

Adding insult to injury, creating OBSF meant spending huge amounts of shareholders' money to structure transactions, just to keep those same shareholders in the dark.

The banker's goal for OBSF was a better-looking balance sheet with a lower reported debt/equity ratio. In reality,

OBSF is simply used to create deliberately misleading financial statements.

But off-balance-sheet financing is a bit like a magic trick, where magicians seem to make things disappear. You know it hasn't really disappeared, but you don't know where it has gone.

America's Lennar Corp., the third-largest US builder by market value, fell 20 per cent in New York trading after a report, which criticised Lennar's practice of putting large amounts of debt in off-balance-sheet transactions, saying there was insufficient disclosure about them to investors. Lennar had about $4 billion in off-balance-sheet debt through 116 joint ventures and had typically given very few details about these arrangements.

The scandal of the US Enron Corporation a few years earlier also involved off-balance-sheet financing. Many of the executives involved were eventually brought to account, parted from their illicit gains and sent to prison.

But what is the real nature of off-balance-sheet trans-actions and how are they constructed? Has the company really reduced its risk by shifting the burden of debt to another company, or has it simply come up with a devious way of visibly eliminating a liability from its balance sheet, but which still exists out of view?

Securitisation

This will be explained in more detail in chapter 6, but a brief explanation is needed here: banks often hold assets, such as mortgages, that third parties might be willing to buy.

To sell the assets, the bank creates a Special Investment Vehicle. The Special Investment Vehicle is then sold as a bond, backed by the income from its assets, in this case, mortgages. The income from the sale of this Special Investment Vehicle/bond is then used to pay the bank for the mortgages it transferred into the Special Investment Vehicle in the first place. The Special Investment Vehicle/ bond then uses the monthly income received from its mortgage holders to give the bond investors a healthy return on their investment. Since much of the credit risk gets offloaded (or so the bankers thought) along with the assets, these liabilities are taken off the banks' balance sheet. This in turn allows the bank to free up capital which would otherwise be tied up in complying with capital adequacy ratios and allow them to make ever riskier and bigger investments.

Banks argue (naturally) that off-balance-sheet techniques benefit investors because they allow management to tap extra sources of financing and reduce liability risk that could hurt earnings. That is partly true, but off-balance-sheet finance also has the power to make companies and their management teams look more competent than they actually are.

In the Irish context, what we do not yet know is who actually invested in these Special Investment Vehicle/bonds. Was it pension funds, over which the banks might have significant control, or perhaps bank in-house property funds?

When shareholders at the Anglo Irish Bank AGM, early in 2009, asked questions of a similar nature to this, they were told by the chairman, 'That's commercially sensitive information.'

Such evasive replies only lead one to believe the worst. The banks needed the Irish taxpayers to accept liability for debts up to a fantastic €485 billion, which illustrates the enormity of the problem these banks had created.

If Irish banks have real liabilities that are not immediately apparent in their companies' financial reports, this runs counter to the banks' fiduciary duty for their shareholders to know the full extent of the banks' liabilities. Unfortunately for all of us, recent evidence has shown that Irish banks seem to have no problem, ethical or otherwise, in knowingly presenting false and misleading information to their investors and shareholders.

Fraud

If fraud is the act of not telling the truth in order to entice others to make decisions they would not make if they knew the truth, then off-balance-sheet financing is tacitly unethical and illegal. But to international investors, such deceptive behaviour chokes off the flow of relevant information in the marketplace, leading them to dump Irish bank shares. This, and not short selling, was the main reason why Irish bank shares collapsed.

Irish bank executives seemed to believe they could secure huge amounts of investment funds by committing legal fraud. But in the end all they succeeded in doing was destroying their banks' credibility and thereby costing their companies far more than they ever gained by this deception.

The Irish Industrial Development Authority (IDA) said in 2007: 'Dublin has established a reputation as a jurisdiction for securitisation that provides a quality service in a regulated environment.' By early 2009, that statement had been well and truly rubbished as it had become evident that Dublin was one of the least regulated financial environments in the world, with catastrophic consequences for the Irish economy.

Today's banking problems began with legislative changes a few years earlier. Bertie Ahern, during his time as Taoiseach, and Brian Cowen, who was Finance Minister during those years, were directly responsible for various pieces of legislation which led to the creation of 'off-balance-sheet' debt as a legitimate business practice.

The Asset Covered Securities Act 2001 established a regime for the issuance of securities (shares) by designated credit institutions; these shares could be secured on pools of mortgage assets, which were separate from the designated credit institution's other creditors.

The Irish Finance Act 2003 dealt with qualifying assets and qualifying company requirements. It said:

> A Qualifying Asset comprised of a financial asset or an interest in a financial asset. A Qualifying Company is a company resident in Ireland that (i) acquires qualifying assets from another person or (ii) as a result of an arrangement with another person holds or manages the qualifying assets or (iii) enters into a legally enforceable agreement with another person that in itself is a qualifying asset.

One of the most damaging aspects of the Finance Act 2003 was that it split the Central Bank from the function of financial regulation.

In the Irish Finance Act 2007, the Irish government abolished stamp duty on the creation and transfer of mortgages and charges executed on or after 7 December 2006.

Irish Special Investment Vehicles were allowed to be established either as limited or unlimited companies under the Companies Acts 2006. Private limited companies were the most common form of business entity used in Ireland, however, many structured finance and securitisation transactions required the use of a public limited company where there was a 'public' offer of securities.

This situation changed in December 2006 when the Investment Funds, Companies and Miscellaneous Provisions Act 2006 (the '2006 Act') was implemented. This Act opened the floodgates on the Irish securitisation market as it allowed private companies to be used for an increased number of transactions.

Historically, private companies were prohibited from making any offer to the public of their shares or debentures. As a result of the 2006 Act, private companies were allowed to offer debt securities which they had been previously been prohibited from doing. The essential features of a private limited company are that the liability of members is limited to the amount of share capital subscribed and that certain obligations imposed on public limited companies do not apply to private limited companies.

One wonders if Messrs Ahern and Cowen realised the full extent of the catastrophe they were unleashing on the Irish economy with the introduction of these pieces of legislation. Probably not. But Ahern, in a professional capacity, is familiar with accountancy procedures. And Cowen is a qualified lawyer, so it's difficult to see how they could not have been aware of the implications.

But revelations in February 2009 by the new Finance Minister Brian Lenihan, also a qualified lawyer, as to how his civil servant advisers kept him in the dark regarding €7 billion in irregular bank transfers between Irish Life & Permanent and Anglo Irish Bank, could easily lead one to believe that crucial pieces of legislation could have been slipped in under the minister's nose without him being fully aware of what was going on. If such a scenario did exist, who exactly was instrumental in bringing this legislation forward?

If Ireland is to rebuild its international financial services reputation it is important to establish precisely who was responsible, as this person, or persons, may still be in positions of power in the finance ministry and their continued presence there will severely impede the restoration of Ireland's financial services reputation for probity.

Ireland, as a matter of urgency, needs to show the international investment community that there is a complete culture change in this important area of our banking standards.

Irish politicians and bank chairmen may dismiss Irish bank shareholders' enquiries with statements like 'that is commercially sensitive information,' but the international investment community will not be dismissed so lightly.

Such stonewalling by the Irish banks to legitimate questions put forward by shareholders who have seen the value of their investments wiped out also creates deep suspicion amongst the same international investment community and will result in the consequent downgrading of our country's sovereign debt. This in turn will lead to vastly increased borrowing costs as our risk profile increases. The international investment community will need to see that the people responsible for the breakdown of the Irish banking system are held to account for their actions. The big problem in this whole area is that the Irish government doesn't 'do' responsibility. This means that there needs to be a culture change within the governing Fianna Fáil party in relation to their attitude to overall acceptable banking and business standards. This will be nearly impossible to achieve as there is a tolerance within that party towards 'likeable' buccaneering corruption. Within Fianna Fáil, property speculator buccaneers have always had a certain gangster charm.

It should be pointed out, of course, that not all Fianna Fáil politicians are tolerant of these types, but sadly such members seem to be in the minority within that party and the buccaneers have bought their way into positions of influence, which has ensured the promotion of their selected party members. This was very well illustrated in the various corruption tribunals over the past ten years.

The practice of securitisation was still going on, long after the Irish taxpayer bailed out the banks in September 2008. This was surely a blatant abuse of the government's guarantee scheme as the banks were simply using it to create still more incredible amounts of debt.

Debt the Irish taxpayers were liable for:

ANGLO IRISH MORTGAGE BANK – €10,000,000,000
Asset Covered Securities Programme   Debt 22/01/2009
Final Terms: Issue of EUR 800,000,000 Floating Rate
Commercial Mortgage Covered Securities due 22 July 2012
(Series 3 Tranche Number 1)   Debt 26/01/2009
Final Terms: Issue of EUR 500,000,000 Floating Rate
Commercial Mortgage Covered Securities due 22 July 2014
(Series 4 Tranche Number 1)   Debt 26/01/2009
Final Terms: Issue of EUR 1,500,000,000 Floating Rate
Commercial Mortgage Covered Securities due 22 January 2011
(Series 1 Tranche Number 1)   Debt 26/01/2009
Final Terms: Issue of EUR 1,000,000,000 Floating Rate
Commercial Mortgage Covered Securities due 22 January 2012
(Series 2 Tranche Number 1)   Debt 26/01/2009

Fitch Ratings, London, 22 January 2009: 'Fitch Ratings has today assigned Anglo Irish Mortgage Bank's (AIMB), "A-" (A minus)/Outlook Stable/"F1+") first Irish commercial mortgage covered securities (MCS) a "AAA" rating. The rating applies to the first four series issued today under the EUR10bn programme for a total combined amount of EUR3.8bn, consisting of series 1, 2, 3, and 4 in amounts of EUR1.5bn, EUR1.0bn, EUR0.8bn, and EUR0.5bn, respectively.'

The bonds have expected due dates of January 2011, January 2012, July 2012, and July 2014 respectively, and benefit from an extended maturity date of eighteen months after the expected due date.

Such a rating from Fitch would not be forthcoming if it were not for the Irish government banking guarantee.

Irish Life & Permanent FASTNET SECURITIES 5 LTD €1.7 billion Mortgage Backed Floating Rate Notes due November 2050   21/10/2008

Irish Life & Permanent FASTNET SECURITIES 6 LTD Mortgage Backed Floating Rate Notes due December 2050   11/11/2008

Start Mortgages, for example, used vehicles called Lansdowne Mortgage Securities (LMS1, LMS2, LMS3). In simple terms, securitisation was a racket used by banks, which turned low-quality mortgages into high-priced derivatives.

In the spring of 2009, long after it ceased in other parts of the world, because nobody would buy them any more, the Irish banks were still out there flogging mortgage-backed securities and they were able to find a market, but only because the government had made the Irish taxpayer liable for all the banks' debts. This was a monumental abuse of Irish taxpayers and, frankly, it beggars belief. The rest of the international investment community must have been looking on in astonishment at what the Irish banks were getting away with.

Chapter 2

THE INSIDERS – BERTIE'S MEN

As March 2009 drew to a close, thousands of Germans took to the streets carrying banners emblazoned with the words 'We won't pay for your banking crisis!' Albert Rupprecht, the chairman of the Bundestag's parliamentary committee overseeing Germany's rescue programme, believed that a commission should identify the people responsible for leaving Germany in its deepest economic crisis since the 1920s and 1930s – and we don't need a history lesson to remember what that crisis led to. Rupprecht felt the commission should have subpoena powers, leading to civil and/or criminal actions in court. The commission, he felt, should include neither bankers nor politicians, no doubt because some of them would eventually end up in the dock.

The German authorities responded swiftly for a reason. The German public was demanding action, and the authorities had genuine fears that the crisis would cause a populist rising and undermine the country's democratic stability. Rupprecht said, 'We do not need a witch hunt nor an inquisition tribunal, but we need to identify who or what was responsible for the crisis. We should not leave it to the populists.' It seems that when the German public wants an explanation for who wrecked their economy, the authorities deem it wise to respond. Quickly.

The Irish people, too, wanted answers early in 2009. However, at the time that this book was going to print, they were still waiting for an honest response from their elected representatives. The Irish citizens have had no say in the way the country has been mismanaged by the government, along with their intimate circle of wealthy friends and the bankers. The Irish public did not ask for the new mortgage legislation introduced in 2003 and 2004, which paved the path for Ireland's present sub-prime property-driven banking crisis. We will look at that in more depth in chapter 4, but first let us look at how Bertie Ahern, as Taoiseach and as Finance Minister, and his close circle of business friends ran the country as they saw fit.

Joe Burke was first appointed chairman of the Dublin Port Company on 25 April 2002. On the last day in office of the FF–PD government in 2007, he was reappointed chairman of the Dublin Port and Docks Board (Dublin Port Company) for a second five-year term, due to run until 2012.

His appointment was among a slew of political postings by Bertie Ahern to state bodies announced on the day after the Dáil was dissolved for the June 2002 general election.

Joe Burke has been amongst the closest of the closed inner circle that surrounded Bertie Ahern since he was first elected to the Dáil in 1977 and he was among the team who moved Bertie Ahern's constituency headquarters from Amiens Street in inner-city Dublin to St Lukes, Drumcondra, in the north of the city.

Joe Burke is also one of the five trustees of Bertie Ahern's constituency headquarters along with the publicly recognised Des Richardson and Tim Collins. The least well-known of the trustees was the late Jimmy Keane, a local 'ward boss' who was a friend of Bertie Ahern's and who guided him through local politics. He remained a largely anonymous figure as did the other trustee, the late Jimmy Kelly.

It was solicitor, trusted legal adviser and friend of Ahern's, Gerry Brennan, who put together the trustee agreement by which Burke, Richardson, Collins, Keane and Kelly agreed to buy, refurbish and fund the St Luke's constituency headquarters. Under the terms of the trusteeship, Bertie Ahern would have the use of the building and facilities for his lifetime in politics and when he retired from politics it would revert to Fianna Fáil.

In May 2008, at the Mahon tribunal, it emerged that Des Richardson was the purchaser of St Luke's. Before tribunal counsel Des O'Neill produced the house purchase contract, Richardson said that he had attended a meeting in the Gresham Hotel in 1987 along with twenty or thirty other people where the purchase of a property was discussed. He told the tribunal he did not have the details of the individual members who contributed to the purchase. He said he might have made a contribution himself, but he didn't have any documentation about it.

Richardson said he was not engaged in the purchase of St Luke's, he did not negotiate the price nor did he open the Cumann O'Donovan Rossa account used to pay for it.

'I was asked to sign the house purchase by our legal adviser [solicitor Gerry Brennan] and on his advice I signed it,' he said.

Solicitor Gerry Brennan committed suicide on 24 May 1997, just days before Bertie Ahern won the election that made him Taoiseach.

The men who set up St Luke's would ensure that Bertie Ahern never had to worry about money and some of them also prospered very substantially in the process. Three of the trustees went on to become multimillionaires and members of important state boards.

Des Richardson was appointed Fianna Fáil chief fund-raiser (1993–1999) by Bertie Ahern when Ahern was appointed party treasurer in 1993. Richardson was also organiser of the infamous tent at the Galway races. In the summer of 2000, Des Richardson had a personal declared net worth of €2.5 million.

Richardson was a businessman with a finger in many pies, in addition to being Fianna Fáil's chief fund-raiser. He was also appointed to the boards of Aer Lingus and the Health and Safety Authority. When appointed to the latter, he set up a company called Workforce and negotiated a contract with Allied Irish Banks to do health and safety surveys for AIB. It was revealed at the Flood Tribunal that, in 1999, Richardson had three jobs, with three separate offices and three salaries. He was getting €70,000 a year as chief fund-raiser for Fianna Fáil, with offices in the exclusive

Berkeley Court Hotel in Dublin. He was executive director at Marlborough Recruitment, with plush offices on Grafton Street, where he earned €70,000 per year. He was also running a consultancy service called Berraway, with registered offices in Upper Mount Street. He was paid more than €100,000 by Berraway in 1999.

Disgraced former lobbyist Frank Dunlop became a shareholder in Berraway in 1992 and remained a shareholder until the company was dissolved in 1999. Berraway's trading address at 25 Upper Mount Street was also the address from which Dunlop's firm, Frank Dunlop & Associates, operated. From August 1996 until early 2000, over €1 million passed through an account held by Berraway.

Des Richardson was also paid a retainer of €1,250 a month to provide 'strategic consultancy' services to multi-millionaire builder and property developer Ken Rohan.

In 1993 and 1994, Rohan launched a strong lobbying campaign with the Minister of Finance, Bertie Ahern, to have the tax laws amended in his favour, in relation to benefit-in-kind tax on his valuable art collection. The Department of Finance urged then Minister Ahern to reject these approaches, in the knowledge that the Revenue Commissioners wanted to pursue Rohan through the courts for a tax judgment that reliable estimates suggested could have been about €2 million as it had to cover a twelve-year period. Ahern overruled the advice of his civil servants. Instead, he passed the legislation and had its effects backdated for twelve years, thereby saving Rohan up to €2 million and around €150,000 per year thereafter.

While in theory it was open to any citizen to benefit from this legislation, Charlie McCreevy, as Minister for Finance, confirmed in the Dáil in 1999 that the only person who qualified was Ken Rohan.

Richardson also established business links with Tim Collins and they became partners in a company called Pilgrim Associates, which provided various services to property firms and developers, and which got a valuable contract from CERT (the state agency providing training for the hotel and tourism industry) when Bertie Ahern was appointed Minister for Labour in 1987.

Tim 'Fixer' Collins is the most interesting of the Drumcondra trustees (or as Charles Haughey called them, 'the Drumcondra Mafia'). He was a Fianna Fáil activist in Dublin Central since the 1970s and worked originally in the tile business. Collins eventually made a fortune from 'putting people together' in very large property deals, in return for a hefty percentage of the profit. Of all of the trustees, he was believed to be the closest to Bertie Ahern. He was appointed to the board of Enterprise Ireland in 1998, after Bertie Ahern was first elected Taoiseach.

In 1998, Collins' fortunes really took off with one particular deal he brokered. The government was interested in acquiring the site of the Battle of the Boyne because of its historical associations. But in December 1997 the McCann family, who control the fruit importers Fyffe's, stepped in and bought the 700-acre site for €2.7 million through a company called Deep River. About a month later, in January 1998, the site was offered to the government. An inter-departmental committee met to discuss buying the land from the McCann's in March 1998. The Office of Public Works (OPW) got a valuation of between €4 million and €7 million as the cost of buying the site.

'It was through the Taoiseach Bertie Ahern's office that we were approached first and we had a formal meeting with his office on March 3, 1999,' said Barry Murphy, then chairman of the OPW. Eighteen months after the land was first mentioned to the OPW, it bought Deep River for €7.8 million. That represented a significant profit of €5.1 million for the already very wealthy McCann family, in a very short time and without having to spend a penny on the deal. Even better, the deal was structured so that the state bought the company Deep River instead of simply buying the land and so the McCanns avoided paying almost €1 million in capital gains tax on the profits of the sale.

Asked was he directed to purchase this land, Murphy of the OPW replied, 'The correct answer to that is that the government asked us to.'

Tim Collins recieved a commission of over €600,000 for himself, very big money back in 1999. He was also rewarded for his services with a job on a government state agency. He was appointed to the board of An Córas Tráchtála (The Export Board) but he resigned before investigations commenced into his business dealings.

Joe Burke

Joe Burke first became friends with Bertie Ahern when they were neighbours thirty years ago. Joe is a frequent doorstep canvasser for Bertie Ahern in his constituency and a member of the fund-raising committee of the O'Donovan Rossa Cumann. Each year the Cumann raised money at an opulent dinner held in the Royal Hospital Kilmainham or Clontarf Castle. In reality this was Bertie Ahern's annual fund-raiser. The dinner was attended by representatives of big business, builders and developers who would take tables at €500 a head. Attendance was by invitation only, with all the proceeds going to paying for a full-time staff, the upkeep of St Luke's and the considerable expense of running Ahern's well-oiled political machine.

Joe Burke first came to public attention during the 'Bertiegate' affair at the end of 2006 when the then Taoiseach Bertie Ahern was forced to reveal that Joe Burke was one of twelve 'close friends' who loaned him the equivalent of €50,000 to pay for costs arising from his marriage break-up.

Joe Burke was born in Donegal in 1950. He was separated from his wife of thirty years and had two adult children. He was a snappy dresser, sporting a €10,000 gold Rolex watch and liked to travel first class.

Many of Joe's close friends were surprised when he began dating a psychologist, Maria Corrigan, who was a Fianna Fáil councillor first elected in 1999. Ms Corrigan, an attractive, professional woman, unsuccessfully contested the Dublin South Dáil seat in 2002 and again in the 2007 general election. After the election, Ms Corrigan was appointed to the Senate as a Taoiseach's nominee.

Between 1985 and 1991, Joe Burke was vice-chairman of Dublin city council's planning committee and also a member of the old Dublin Port and Docks Board.

In 1989, after developer Tom Gilmartin complained to Ahern (who was then Minister for Labour) about his difficulties in progressing plans for a huge shopping centre at Quarryvale in west Dublin, it was Joe Burke whom Bertie Ahern sent to meet Gilmartin. Ahern insisted in his evidence to the planning tribunal that this was the only meeting Joe Burke had with the developer, and he said Joe Burke was 'quite adamant that he did not ask him for or about a contribution to Fianna Fáil, at my behest or otherwise'.

In October 1997, a man named Philip Sheedy was jailed for four years for killing Anne Ryan, a Tallaght mother of two young children, as a result of drunken driving. Philip Sheedy had worked as an architect for Joe Burke's construction business. Sheedy spent six months in Mountjoy Jail and was then transferred to the more salubrious surroundings of Shelton Abbey.

On 14 October 1998, Joe Burke visited Sheedy in Shelton Abbey. A few weeks later, the Sheedy case was re-listed and he was released from prison.

Both Supreme Court judge Hugh O'Flaherty and the judge who released Philip Sheedy, Cyril Kelly, resigned as a result of the scandal that occurred when these facts were revealed.

Then Taoiseach Bertie Ahern, in July 1998, asked the then Minister for Justice whether it would be possible for Sheedy to get day release. The Taoiseach's inquiry was recorded in a written note to his secretary, to which she testified at a subsequent tribunal inquiry.

Bertie Ahern said: 'I applied no political pressure to get Mr Sheedy's early release.'

The episode ended Justice Hugh O'Flaherty's career on the bench and he had been widely tipped as the next President of the Supreme Court.

Dublin Port Company

Dublin Port was incorporated as a limited liability company in 1997, the Minister for the Marine being its sole shareholder on behalf of the state. Unlike its semi-state neighbour, the Dublin Docklands Authority, and unlike most other state bodies, Dublin Port Company is not subject to the Freedom of Information Act and therefore has no statutory obligation to provide certain information about itself.

Some of Ireland's richest property developers are involved in developing Dublin Port Company real estate. Philip Lynch's One51, which has a significant shareholding in both ICG (parent company of Irish Ferries, which has a thirty-acre lease in the port) and NTR (National Toll Roads) bought Greenore port in County Louth in partnership with Dublin Port Company. The company's board approved the sale by tender of Balbriggan and Skerries harbours in March 2004, but it was overruled by ministerial order after a number of cross-party TDs in north Dublin protested. After behind-the-scenes representations were made to the government, the harbours were handed over to Fingal County Council by order of the then minister, Dermot Ahern, under Section 88 of the Harbours Act 1996.

€412-million dock site sale

The Irish Glass Bottle Company, later renamed Ardagh, ceased production on a site it leased in Ringsend from Joe Burke's Dublin Port Company.

The site lease was then purchased by a company called South Wharf. In 2005, South Wharf lost a High Court case that resulted from Dublin Port Company's refusal to allow it to change the site use from manufacturing and warehousing.

After the High Court case, South Wharf turned around and joined with the Dublin Port Company to redevelop the property, which then was rezoned to permit commercial, residential and retail use. Joe Burke's firm, Dublin Port Company, got a third share of South Wharf for this purpose.

South Wharf then decided to sell the company rather than develop the site. A consortium named Becbay was the highest bidder, at €412 million.

Developer and former Clare Fianna Fáil county councillor Bernard McNamara owned 41 per cent of Becbay, while investor and former Revenue inspector Derek Quinlan had a 33 per cent stake through his company Mempal Limited. The Dublin Docklands Development Authority held the remaining 26 per cent.

Chairman of Dublin Docklands Development Authority at the time was Lar Bradshaw of Anglo Irish Bank and originator of the deal, Sean Fitzpatrick, was also on the board.

When Fitzpatrick led the Dublin Docklands Development Authority into this €412-million land deal, he was simultaneously a member of the state company's Finance, Audit, Risk and Remuneration Committees. Sean Fitzpatrick had been appointed to the Dublin Docklands Development

Authority in 1998 by then Fianna Fáil Environment Minister, Noel Dempsey.

Under the deal South Wharf shareholders would receive €273.5 million, with €138.5 million being paid to Joe Burke's 'Dublin Port Company'.

What makes this deal so worrying now for the Irish taxpayer is the huge level of debt inside the winning Becbay consortium. For example, Bernard McNamara put in €57.5 million for a 41 per cent stake but only €5 million in cash. The balance came from Davy Stockbrokers clients who subscribed for loan stock. In return they were to get a very high 17 per cent per annum return, which illustrated the perceived level of risk in the project.

This was mainly owing to the fact that the original purchase was backed by a €288-million loan from Anglo Irish Bank. The Dublin Docklands Development Authority itself had put up over €32 million cash, presumably borrowed, while the latest annual report for the Authority also reveals loans to joint venture undertakings of €37.6 million, €32.8 million of which is accounted for by 'unsecured interest-free' loans to Becbay.

The notes to the accounts state 'the executive board is satisfied that Becbay Ltd will not be required to repay this debt in the short-term and therefore these loans have been classified as financial assets'.

It is very difficult to understand why the board allowed the Dublin Docklands Development Authority to become involved in such a high-risk and potentially costly situation.

Fine Gael front bencher Phil Hogan, of the Oireachtas Environment Committee, questioned senior executives of the

Dublin Docklands Development Authority on the Irish Glass Bottle land deal. Hogan is looking for a valuation of the 26-acre South Wharf site to be carried out by an 'independent valuer who has no association with a financial institution'.

The Dublin Docklands Development Authority chief executive Paul Maloney said he expects the site to be written down by about 30 per cent, a claim that is dismissed as 'ridiculous' by professional land experts. Valuations of the site from land experts value it at about €100 million in the current market, meaning the site has lost about €300 million, or 75 per cent, in value since it was purchased. The Irish taxpayer will now be liable for this loss as the current government gave a blanket guarantee on all bank debts.

In February 2009, the Dublin Docklands Development Authority revealed that Becbay, the vehicle that acquired the site, has not been paying interest on the loan on the land, pending a renegotiation of terms, since the second half of 2008. Phil Hogan said former Dublin Docklands Development Authority chairman and Anglo Irish Bank director Lar Bradshaw 'did not declare a conflict of interest' in relation to the fact that he was a client of Quinlan's private wealth management business. Dublin Docklands Development Authority chief executive Maloney also confirmed that Bradshaw did not declare his business relationship with Paul Coulson, the main person behind South Wharf, who sold the Poolbeg site. Phil Hogan said Bradshaw had a business relationship through a company, Balcuik, with Paul Coulson, the principal, with Joe Burke's Dublin Port Company, of South Wharf which was selling the IGB site to the Dublin Docklands Development Authority.

Donal O'Connor, current chairman of Anglo Irish Bank, is formerly chairman of Dublin Docklands Development Authority.

Joe Burke restriction order

Joe Burke's pub-renovation company, J&H Burke & Son Builders Ltd, went into liquidation in 2007, having been incorporated in 1995 and filed its last accounts for 2003.

In November 2008, a High Court judge found Burke was 'irresponsible' in the way he ran his own building firm. The liquidator of Burke's company applied to have Burke banned as a director.

Mr Justice Kevin Feeney made a restriction order, under Section 150 of the Companies Acts, because Burke had not acted responsibly in relation to the affairs of his building company. But the judge also found that Burke had acted irresponsibly in not arranging for the preparation and filing of accounts, including audited accounts, for the company for 2004 and 2005. The judge said he acted irresponsibly in failing to inquire about the true financial position of the company and in allowing the company to trade and build up tax debts when it was insolvent.

The judge said the company was insolvent from August 2004 on.

By the end of 2006, the company had accumulated losses of more than €900,000 with about half of that amount owed to Burke. The judge added there was no question of any lack of honesty by Burke who also acted honourably in ensuring employees were paid.

Earlier in 2008, similar restriction orders were made, on an uncontested basis, against Helen Burke, Burke's estranged wife and former financial controller of the firm, and against Brendan O'Reilly, a former director and operations manager of the firm.

The High Court judgment was now going to impact Joe Burke's chairmanship of the Dublin Port Company, as Paragraph 1.2 of the Dublin Port Director's Code of Conduct says:

> It is expected that the directors of the company will apply the same duty and care to the resources of the company as they would to their own resources. The ethos should be strongly focused on the principles of control and integrity.

At the end of January 2009, Joe Burke resigned as executive chairman of Dublin Port Company.

Chapter 3

THE CELTIC TIGER – WHAT WAS IT EXACTLY?

The phrase 'Tiger economies' was first used to describe the 'East Asian Tigers' of South Korea, Singapore, Hong Kong, and Taiwan, during their periods of rapid growth in the 1980s and 1990s. The term 'Celtic Tiger' has been used to refer to Ireland's boom years. The first recorded use of the phrase is in a 1994 Morgan Stanley report by UK economist Kevin Gardiner; he coined the term 'Celtic Tiger', comparing Ireland's economy to the Asian tiger economies (Kevin Gardiner, 'The Irish Economy: a Celtic tiger', MS *Euroletter*, 31 August 1994). Ireland's Celtic Tiger period of rapid growth occurred from the mid 1990s to 2007.

Credit for this period of dramatic growth is generally given to:

- EU membership
- Low corporation tax

- English-speaking workforce
- Foreign direct investment
- Investment in higher education
- State-driven economic development
- Social partnership between employers, government and unions

In September 2008, Ireland became the first Eurozone country to officially fall into recession. The recession was confirmed by figures from the Central Statistics Office which signalled the end of the property boom and a collapse in consumer spending. The Celtic Tiger was dead.

2007 – Just one year earlier

Bank of Ireland declared that Ireland was the world's wealthiest nation after Japan. They said at that stage we had 33,000 millionaires in Ireland.

Bank of Ireland 'Private Banking' published its annual 'Wealth of the Nation' report, which showed that Ireland's net wealth grew by 19 per cent to €805 billion in 2006, one of the fastest growth rates in a survey of the eight leading OECD nations. It said the average wealth per head stood at €196,000 compared to €168,000 the previous year. The report examined Ireland's wealth as measured by assets such as property, deposits and investments. It discovered that the Irish household finances were in excellent health with asset values ahead of liabilities by a factor of six, with gross assets of €964 billion against household liabilities of €161 billion.

In 2006, net assets were €804 billion and this was forecast to increase to €928 billion in 2010 and €1.2 billion in 2015.

Pat O'Sullivan, Senior Economist with Bank of Ireland Private Banking, the report's author, said:

> Last year [2007] was a stellar one for wealth creation in Ireland with net wealth growing by 19 per cent. Strong economic growth combined with a strong performance by domestic and international asset markets resulted in a significant increase in Irish household wealth.
>
> Unsurprisingly, the vast bulk of this wealth was driven by the domestic residential market, although other assets also saw strong increases, ranging from property at 20 per cent growth, investment funds at 18 per cent and pension funds at 11 per cent. Despite the continued high level of debt accumulation, which grew by 21 per cent, the household balance sheet remains very robust with assets outnumbering liabilities by a multiple of six.
>
> Our original forecasts for the wealth of the domestic household remain on track, and we expect net assets to increase to €1.2 trillion by 2015, an increase of 80 per cent in the coming decade.

In 2006, Irish asset division stood at: cash 10 per cent, bonds 3 per cent, equities 16 per cent and property 72 per cent. By 2015, the report predicted that asset division would change to: cash 12 per cent, bonds 5 per cent, equities 22 per cent and property 61 per cent. The report outlined that

Ireland's personal disposal income had doubled over the previous ten years, and this would double again over the next ten years. The annual level of personal savings stood at €10 billion at the end of 2006 and this would increase to €13.5 billion by 2010 and to €24 billion by 2015. This equalled 14 per cent of disposable income. Only Germany's savings level, which was around 10 per cent, approached ours.

The report estimated that there was an increase of 10 per cent in the number of millionaires in Ireland, from 30,000 to 33,000, in the twelve months. The definition of a millionaire by Bank of Ireland Private Banking is the sum of total assets excluding principal private residence. They estimated that there were approximately 330 such individuals with a net worth of over €30 million, 3,000 more with a net worth between €5 million and €30 million and the remainder having a net worth of €1 million to €5 million.

At the launch of the report, Mark Cunningham, Managing Director, Bank of Ireland Private Banking, explained the impact of this increased wealth on the Bank's Private Banking business thus:

> Private Banking has grown exponentially in response to wider wealth creation trends in Ireland with our sales volumes increasing by 30 per cent year on year in 2006. So far this year, we have seen a continuation of strong investment flows and perhaps the beginnings of a much greater diversity in the areas in which Irish investors are looking to deploy wealth. In response to the increasing customer sophistication and growth in

demand, we have expanded the breadth of our offering, re-affirming our position as the country's leading private bank.'

The Celtic Tiger dies

Twenty-four months after this report was written we had officially fallen into recession and by December 2008, Anglo Irish Bank, Bank of Ireland and Allied Irish Bank were ejected from the FTSEurofirst 300 Index of top European shares, following a 90 per cent collapse in the banks' share prices and the resulting loss of market capitalisation.

At the same time, ratings agency Standard & Poor's downgraded the country's banking risk assessment to reflect the rising economic risk in Ireland and the expected continued deterioration in the health of our banks.

The banks then asked the government if it would bail them out by covering their depositors' funds with a guarantee. The government agreed. Then the banks also asked if they could transfer liability for all their debts over to the Irish taxpayers, up to a level of €485 billion. Amazingly, the government agreed to this also. The government sold the deal to the Irish taxpayer by saying this action was necessary 'to prevent the collapse of Ireland's entire financial system'.

Why did things go so terribly wrong, just twenty-four months after the Bank of Ireland's hugely optimistic report was written?

The most negative contribution was made by government policy decisions, which fuelled the housing bubble. Tax incentives were introduced, which prompted a buying binge, which in turn further increased both house prices and the numbers of houses being built. This led to the cost of an average house increasing 300 per cent in ten years.

Housing investment had grown to 14 per cent of Ireland's economy by 2006, three times the European average. In the six years from 2001 to 2006, the government had also increased public sector salaries (including their own) by 59 per cent. During this period, banks made profits, mainly from the property and construction sector, of billions each year and bank executives creamed off incredible bonuses.

Our government and banking leaders were all hell-bent on flogging the Celtic Tiger to death, with no thought of tomorrow.

In 2004, former Taoiseach Charles J. Haughey described the then Fianna Fáil/PD coalition headed by Bertie Ahern, as 'the worst government in the history of the state. The worst, they can't seem to get anything right and have no real vision of the future of Ireland.'

These proved to be very prophetic words indeed.

The boom is now rapidly deflating, which is leading to soaring unemployment, declining consumer spending, a banking sector which is in a mess, businesses going to the wall and the spectre of immigration rearing its head once more as the only option for the youth of Ireland.

During the boom period, the hugely excessive pay rises our government awarded to public sector workers saddled Ireland with a public sector salaries and pensions bill of €18.6 billion by 2008. This accounted for 38 per cent of all government spending. At the end of 2008, the public sector had been promised even more salary increases during 2009.

This huge public sector wage bill is now the single greatest burden on the Irish taxpayer and will be the greatest impediment to our economic recovery.

Since he resigned as Taoiseach, Bertie Ahern has been getting a pension of €164,000 per year. In addition, he continues to collect his TD's salary of €106,567 per year. So Bertie Ahern is currently being paid €5,650 per week by the Irish taxpayers, plus expenses and a chauffeur-driven Mercedes.

Meanwhile, a third of a million (and rising rapidly) Irish people are unemployed and surviving on €200 per week dole money. This is neither right nor just.

Our huge public sector pay bill is also causing Ireland to become less competitive for international investors. US subsidiaries in Ireland employ around 100,000 people. In 2006, America provided a third of all inward investment into Irish manufacturing.

Many of these multinational companies, who were the foundation of our original prosperity, are now considering leaving Ireland. Dell Computers, for example began cutting thousands of jobs at its Limerick plant early in 2009. Many more multinationals have signalled that they, too, will be shedding jobs.

We have survived downturns before, but this one is going to play out differently.

The full extent of the housing collapse is not yet clear, and the commercial property sector will be next to default. This will affect retail outlets, shopping malls and hotels nationwide. The first signs of this coming whirlwind were the 50 per cent SALE announcements *before* Christmas. Retail rents increased dramatically over the past five years to the extent that Grafton Street in Dublin is now one of the most expensive shopping streets in the world. Similar unsustainable rent increases have occurred, to a lesser extent, in all towns around the country. Unlike home mortgages, commercial mortgages are generally for periods of five or ten years with big payments due at the end. When the downturn hits the commercial property sector, those same retailers will not be able to afford the rent, which was expected to cover their landlord's mortgage payments.

Major UK retail chains, who have numerous outlets in Ireland, were already indicating at the end of 2008 that they would be seeking bankruptcy protection in 2009. The closure of the Woolworths chain over Christmas was a major indicator of this development.

Ireland's retail sector faces major lay-offs in 2009.

Chapter 4

2003 AND 2004 – THE CRITICAL YEARS

As events began to unfold early in 2009, it was becoming clearer by the day that the Irish economy was in very bad shape and had been very badly managed over the previous five years. It was becoming more evident with each passing day that Bertie Ahern's government over that ten-year period had lacked both the vision and competence necessary to take maximum advantage of Ireland's temporary economic boom. It was a system of government with limited accountability, where the buck stops with nobody. Hundreds of millions of euro in public funds could be squandered and both ministers and senior public servants would deny any responsibility. Public sector pay and pensions had been increased to an exorbitantly unsustainable level, while over 1 million Irish private sector workers had no occupational pensions to rely on in their old age.

So here we were in early 2009, after ten years of unprecedented prosperity, and we didn't even have a workable national internet broadband network.

The boards of directors and senior management at Ireland's banks had brought their businesses to the verge of ruin, only being saved by the Irish taxpayers accepting liability for their debts. Property-related activities accounted for almost two-thirds of outstanding private sector bank lending.

It appeared (because nobody will give the real figures) that 80 per cent of Anglo Irish Bank's €68-billion loan book, i.e. just under €55 billion, was secured against Irish and British property. It also appeared that Bank of Ireland's loan book stood at €135 billion, 71 per cent (or €95 billion) secured against property, and that AIB's loan book topped €150 billion, with about 60 per cent secured against property.

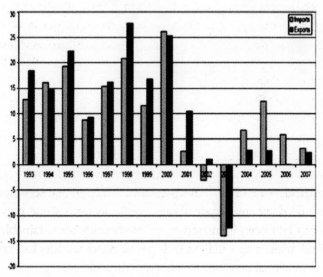

Ireland's Percentage Growth in Imports & Exports 1993–2007 (Labour party)

Could something have been done to avoid the catastrophe which had now befallen the Irish economy?

Yes, and this is very clearly illustrated in the chart on the previous page. The chart below graphically shows how the situation declined dramatically in comparison to the previous five years – and would have been apparent to anyone monitoring the data. It shows that a critical point had been reached and not some minor blip that could have been easily overlooked.

The key moment for the Irish economy was 2003–2004. That was when our exports fell away and our current account deficit plummeted. This was also when Ireland lost its

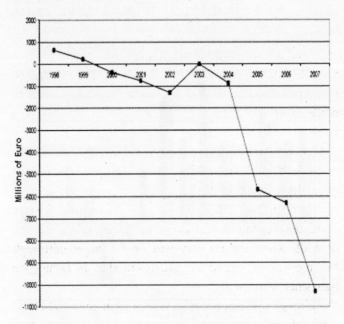

Ireland's Balance of Payments on Current Account 1998–2007 (Labour party).

Finance Minister Charlie McCreevy, the man many credited with doing much to foster the growth of the Celtic Tiger boom. As Minister for Finance (1997–2004), McCreevy had introduced a number of innovations which greatly assisted the creation of Ireland's period of wealth and prosperity. He was also viewed as actively pro-enterprise, anti-spending and a key advocate for tax cuts. He halved capital gains tax from 40 per cent to 20 per cent. He introduced the very successful SSIA savings scheme.

In the early 2000s, when Irish economic growth declined, he maintained strict control on growth in government spending. He maintained a surplus during his seven years in Finance, while also implementing a tax-cutting programme and major increases in health and education. In addition, he increased investment in infrastructural development to 5 per cent of GNP. Unemployment was reduced from 10 per cent to 4.4 per cent. Real GDP growth during McCreevy's time in office represented the highest average of any western European country.

McCreevy was known as a straight talker. He once referred to the Irish health system as a 'black hole' and reacted to the initial Irish rejection of the Lisbon Treaty as 'a sign of a healthy democracy'. He set up the National Pensions Reserve Fund, the contents of which were very valuable in the spring of 2009 when the country was on its knees (although McCreevy never wanted the contents used in the fashion we have since witnessed).

Although one can never be sure of what goes on behind closed doors, our political sources reliably inform us that, in 2003, McCreevy was in direct conflict with his Taoiseach Bertie Ahern with regard to the future direction of economic policy. McCreevy, apparently, wanted to rein in the economy at that point, which in hindsight was the correct course of action, but the Taoiseach wanted the opposite. Bertie Ahern wanted more property-related tax breaks to further fuel the already overheated construction and housing sectors.

Ahern won out and Brian Cowen replaced Charlie McCreevy as Finance Minister.

Cowen then did Ahern's bidding – with disastrous consequences for the Irish economy. It was allowed to develop into an out-of-control property boom, rather than focusing on developing a domestic exporting sector. Between 2000 and 2007, employment in Ireland expanded by 40 per cent – in construction, public services, retail and distribution – while employment in the international tradeable goods and services sector actually fell.

At the end of February 2009, Charlie McCreevy called on the government to produce a detailed plan of economic policy for the next several years. McCreevy said that such a plan was needed to help maintain international confidence in Ireland and it was also essential that taxes on capital and work remained competitive. 'That will require a detailed and credible plan for reducing our indebtedness by laying out how, over a three- to four-year period, we intend to close the formidable gap between government income and spending,' he said. He added that Ireland also needed to rebuild its competitiveness. 'That's not just about reducing costs, although being realistic about our living standards in the new economic circumstances is important. But it is much more about reducing our unit costs, and we can do that by increasing our productivity and efficiency – in public and private sector alike.'

He said no one wants a divide to open up between the public and private sector. 'When the tide turns back in this country's favour, I want the public sector to share in the prosperity that that tide will create. But, in particular, I want the public sector to share in the sustainable efficiencies and cost savings that they themselves generate through higher productivity and more flexible working and recruitment practices,' he said.

He added that, around the world, capital available for governments to borrow had never been so scarce. 'So it stands to reason that governments that bring forward the best-laid, the most detailed, and most credible plans for getting their budgets back to balance will be the governments that attract the capital at a sensible price; others will pay a hefty premium if, indeed, the capital is available at all. Ireland, with its substantial national pension reserve fund and currently low debt-to-GDP ratio, is in one sense well-placed. But in another sense we are hugely challenged, because of the size of the gap between revenue and expenditure that has now opened up. The government had no choice but to start facing up to this issue. To have dodged or delayed the decision would have had consequences that would have made the recent and pending cutbacks seem like a walk in the park,' he said.

In total, 86,000 jobs were created in 2006, according to the Central Statistics Office. Construction accounted for

28,400 and the Health Service Executive 18,700. Only 6,000 jobs were created in the tradeable goods/services sector of the economy, according to policy advisory agency Forfás. The construction sector employed 126,100 in 1998 and 282,000 by the end of 2006 when housing output peaked at 92,000 units.

In November 2004, the then Finance Minister Brian Cowen disclosed that the state collected 28 per cent of the cost of each new house in taxes and public charges. The state was collecting an average of €100,000 from every housing unit built.

In 2003, Irish site costs accounted for 42.5 per cent of the cost of a house nationwide. During the same period, in Denmark and the US the figure was 20 per cent and in Portugal it was 15 per cent.

Also during this period the National Roads Authority was engaged in building extensive new road networks through-out Ireland, which required the purchase of land from farmers all over the country. Land accounted for 23 per cent of the cost of roads projects in Ireland, 12 per cent in England, 10 per cent in Denmark and 9 per cent in Greece.

The Central Statistics Office reported that there were 266,000 vacant dwellings in Ireland in 2006 representing 15 per cent of the total housing stock. Of these, 175,000 were houses, 42,000 were flats and 50,000 were classified as holiday homes.

In Scottish economist Adam Smith's famous book, *The Wealth of Nations*, published in in 1776, he wrote:

> A dwelling house, as such, contributes nothing to the revenue of its inhabitant; and though it is, no doubt,

extremely useful to him, it is as his clothes and household furniture are useful to him, which, however, makes a part of his expense, and not of his revenue. If it is to be let to a tenant for rent, as the house itself can produce nothing, the tenant must always pay the rent out of some other revenue which he derives either from labour, or stock, or land. Though a house, therefore, may yield a revenue to its proprietor, and thereby serve in the function of a capital to him, it cannot yield any to the public, nor serve in the function of a capital to it, and the revenue of the whole body of the people can never be in the smallest degree increased by it.

We are also reliably informed that, in 2003, Charlie McCreevy had a fundamental difference of opinion with Bertie Ahern regarding the separation of the function of financial regulation from the Central Bank. Again, McCreevy lost this argument, which culminated in the passing of the Central Bank and Financial Services Authority of Ireland Bill 2003. This became known as the Irish Financial Services Regulatory (IFSR) Act.

The new Office of the Financial Services Regulator was established on 1 May 2003. This was reputed to have heralded the final break between Charlie McCreevy and Bertie Ahern. McCreevy went on to replace David Byrne as Ireland's European Commissioner in 2004.

If remedial action had been taken during the 2003–2004 period, Ireland would not have experienced anything like the mess it subsequently found itself in. Of course, the politicians will say '*hindsight is a great thing,*' but Bertie Ahern and Brian Cowen were leading the country at that time and they allowed the economic situation to get totally out of hand, and the Irish people are now suffering for their bad judgment and leadership during the period.

The Irish people have been conned. They have been duped by serpent-tongued, self-serving politicians and bankers. By 2005, the economy was beginning to come under strain, but the government needed consumers to carry on spending in order to keep taxes flowing. The method chosen was simple. Create an enormous housing bubble, convince consumers that it made sense to borrow money against the rising value of their homes and everything would be okay.

The banks joined in the fun with mortgage securitisation mania. Vast quantities of Monopoly money were changing hands even though those involved in the deals had no idea of their real worth. Not that they cared. Inevitably, the bubble burst and the huge banking securitisation racket had been exposed for what it is – a racket.

Banks brought themselves down with poor decision making and short-term greed and very nearly brought down the country's financial system, and may yet do so. How can the employees of these companies be still entitled to multimillion-euro bonuses?

As the daily job losses continue to grow at a staggering rate, as the damage to the economy deepens, as past bank 'earnings' on which bank executives' compensation was calculated have proved to be nothing more than smoke and mirrors, as taxpayers are taken to the cleaners again and again, there must surely be a very strong case for a clawback of these funds.

When the state bailed out the Irish banking sector, new regulations should have been put in place governing the obscene bonuses and paydays which, by right, should be classed as 'fraudulent transfers'.

Had such measures been taken, the Minister for Finance could then take the necessary legal steps to assure that such funds be returned to the banks' 'estate' and their creditors, who are now in large measure the Irish taxpayers. Instead, what we appear to be doing by keeping the banks out of bankruptcy is shielding extravagant pay packages from the legal demands of a receiver.

The question of bank bonuses was best summed up by Boris Johnson, the Mayor of London, who said, 'Giving bankers bonuses is the same as giving Lord Cardigan a bonus for the Charge of the Light Brigade.'

Economic mismanagement

One of Ireland's great mistakes during the boom years is that our government never built up any reserves. Singapore, with whom we are often compared in relation to the size of its economy, managed to build up a reserve fund of €170 billion over this period.

The other grave mistake our government made was to fuel the building of houses long after demand had dried up. Consequently, we now have a huge overhang of unsold housing which will delay our recovery for many years. This situation is further exacerbated by the emigration of many of our young people who would be expected to take up this excess housing supply in the coming years.

However unpalatable for our property speculators and their banker partners, these houses will need to be drastically marked down in price to remove the backlog and allow the construction sector to get moving again.

Chapter 5

THE BANKS – THEY GAMBLED AND LOST

I rish banks have gone from being the most valuable businesses in the country in 2006 to being practically worthless by the end of 2008. In fact, if they had not been bailed out by the Irish taxpayer, most major Irish banks would have been bankrupt by the end of 2008.

If one accepts the notion that bankers had a fiduciary obligation to their shareholders, then we need to point out that the duties of a fiduciary include 'loyalty and reasonable care of the assets within its custody.'

A person acting in a fiduciary capacity is required to make truthful and complete disclosures to those placing trust in him/her.

Anglo Irish Bank and Irish Life & Permanent have certainly not been open and/or transparent in the way they transferred vast sums of money, clearly hiding the true state of their finances from their shareholders and any potential new investors. Have individuals within those banks been engaged in fraud and deceit, breach of fiduciary duty, civil conspiracy to commit fraud and gross negligence? It will be interesting to see if anyone is found responsible. If the matter is washed over, then confidence in both banking and justice will fade further, and our economy will go into a downward spiral from which it will take years to recover.

In the early years of this decade, Ireland got a shot at the big time. We were allowed into the Eurozone, which gave us a currency as strong as that of Germany, with its attendant low interest rates. It now appears that as a result of economic and political corruption the government has squandered this once-in-a-lifetime opportunity for our country to compete on level terms with the great nations of the world.

Some Irish bank executives have been involved in fraud on a massive scale. Anglo Irish Bank, with the collusion of Irish Life & Permanent, fraudulently misled shareholders and investors as to the true level of customer deposits in Anglo Irish.

On 30 September 2008, Irish Life & Permanent deposited €4 billion (that's right: four thousand million euro) in Anglo Irish Bank, and Irish Life & Permanent colluded in an underhanded and deceitful mechanism to make it appear as if this €4 billion was normal depositors' funds. This action will open up both Anglo Irish Bank and Irish Life & Permanent to massive lawsuits.

The previous day, 29 September 2008, the Irish government gave a blanket guarantee which covered loans of €485 billion in the Irish banking system. The juxtapositioning of the government's guarantee and the irregular Irish Life/ Anglo Irish transaction must raise questions about the information passing between the banks, the Taoiseach Brian Cowen and Finance Minister Brian Lenihan. Either the government knew and tried to hide the facts to protect the 'credibility' of Irish banking, in which case they were stupid to think we wouldn't find out. Or they did not know, which means they had not done their homework before signing up generations of Irish taxpayers as involuntary guarantors over an unfathomable debt.

Stupid or reckless? The truth will probably only become evident in the months and years ahead. When this transaction was made public, not, I might add, by the Finance Minister or the Financial Regulator but by the *Sunday Business Post* newspaper, the Irish Life chairman Gillian Bowler said, 'The intention was to support the policy objective of the Financial Regulator'.

Needless to say, the Financial Regulator immediately announced that Irish Life was not telling the truth about the matter and that he at no time encouraged them, or any other bank, to engage in fraud.

When the Finance Minister eventually forced Casey, Irish Life chief executive, to resign, the Irish Life chairman Ms Bowler said he was a man of 'the highest integrity'. Perhaps, but it would seem that Irish Life itself did not share that depth of integrity.

This sharp practice on the part of the Irish banks has come as a huge shock to Irish consumer confidence and their belief in the integrity of the banking system. The main board directors and senior management of our banks stand in disgrace for having allowed the collapse of the Irish banking system under their watch and it will take a long time before ordinary Irish people trust the bankers again, and that is a very damaging situation for the economy as a whole.

It will make the current recession far deeper and more damaging than any which have gone before. This banking crisis will continue to affect Ireland's economy negatively for years to come and those fantasists who predict a recovery 'in the latter part of 2009, or early 2010' are in for a very severe reality check.

Is the current Irish government serious about attempting to rehabilitate the Irish banking system? Consider the following and you be the judge.

At the beginning of February 2009, US President Barack Obama decreed that no bank which received government help could pay any of its executives more than $500,000 (€385,000) per year.

Taoiseach Brian Cowen and Finance Minister Brian Lenihan then said they were going to have a similar review of Irish bank executives' pay. They could have made a simple decision like the President of the US and said 'any Irish banks who avail of Irish taxpayers' funds must cap executive pay at €385,000 ($500,000) per annum'. That would be very simple and it could be reasonably argued that what was good enough for US banks would also work well for Ireland, even though in reality we should probably look to pay our bank executives much less than the US does as our banks are minuscule in size by comparison.

But that's not what Brian Cowen's government did. Instead they appointed consultants named 'Covered

Institution Remuneration Oversight Committee' (CIROC), to advise on how much Irish bank executives should be paid. It then transpired that one of the three consultants tasked with this job is a lady named Vivienne Jupp. In October 2007, Vivienne Jupp was a key member of the six-person Review Body on Higher Remuneration in the Public Sector which decided that the then Taoiseach, Bertie Ahern, should receive a 14 per cent pay rise, which would have increased his annual salary by €38,000 per annum to €310,000, or €6,458 per week. This would have made Bertie Ahern the highest paid leader in the world.

In early 2008, after becoming Taoiseach, Brian Cowen was asked if he would defer this €38,000 increase and he replied 'it would be hypocritical not to accept it'. So do you really think this government is serious about reforming the Irish banking system? Incidentally, the CIROC consultancy is chaired by a man named Eddie Sullivan, who is a former secretary general with the Department of Finance. The third member of the CIROC team is former Comptroller and Auditor General, John Purcell, who retired in May 2008.

One of the most obvious lessons of this crisis is that both capital and customer deposits are much more precious than many of our bankers seemed to have realised.

The huge profits of Irish banks, over the past five years, were driven by unsustainable risk-taking and very dangerous degrees of leverage. The bankers now need to find a new way of operating which will restore their businesses to profitability. This will be extremely difficult to achieve and failure will be a constant threat.

While the bankers are getting on with that, our government needs to establish accountability within the banking community for the causes of the current crisis. Decisions were taken by banking directors and senior management here in Ireland, which caused these companies to be run into the ground and those responsible should be identified and held to account. How this matter is prosecuted will be of vital importance to Ireland's international reputation. It will send clear signals as to what is acceptable business practice in Ireland and what is not. If any of our laws have been broken, those responsible will have to be punished this time. There should be no attempt to turn this into another long-drawn-out and outrageously expensive tribunal circus. This time it should be conducted as a straightforward fraud investigation, conducted by the Garda Fraud Squad and the Criminal Assets Bureau. The situation, to date, is that the Irish taxpayers have been compelled, by the government, to accept liability for bank debts up to €485 billion. These debts are the result of reckless behaviour by an elite and very wealthy class.

Do the banks stand accused of knowingly providing 100 per cent mortgage debt to borrowers whom they must have known were going to default, especially as some of those loans were for seven times the borrowers' income? In the US, the FBI is conducting investigations into their mortgage providers and they estimate that as many as 70 per cent of borrowers who defaulted on their loans 'significantly misrepresented information' on their loan applications. This represents negligence and a lack of proper due diligence by the loan providers. The FBI is also looking into the sales practices employed in the marketing of these mortgages.

The banks knew the risks they were taking on. They camouflaged these risks by moving the debts off balance sheet and in the process removing a liability from their balance sheets. The banks were in effect 'hiding' their risky debt. This practice would seem to be at odds with the legal requirement of a person *'acting in a fiduciary capacity'*. Such a person is required 'to make truthful and complete disclosures to those placing trust in him'. If the bankers claim that they did not believe they had a fiduciary obligation to their shareholders then that reveals an even more appalling vista. This off-balance-sheet debt manoeuvre also had the effect of making the bank directors and their management teams look far more competent than they actually were. (See also chapter 7).

In 2002, the US Enron Corporation collapsed under a weight of debt and accounting fraud involving a network of off-balance-sheet companies. Many of the executives involved were eventually brought to account, parted from their illicit gains and sent to prison.

There will be huge anger in Ireland if many of the rapacious bankers whose behaviour contributed enormously to triggering the current crisis are going to be allowed off scot-free, to retire to their mansions and yachts with their fantastic fortunes intact.

There should be no sympathy for bankers who have run their companies into the ground by taking on dangerous levels of risk, because they had the resources to weigh up the risks they were taking on. Investors purchased stock in these banks only to see their values collapse. They lost their life savings as the bank stocks were very risky and not a prudent investment, contrary to what the banks themselves had said at the time. As late as August 2008 Irish banks were telling investors that everything was rosy and there was no need to worry. The banks have since turned in losses they failed to anticipate or fully account for and watched their share values collapse by 95 per cent. Failure by the banks to disclose material information, by hiding it off balance sheet, prevented the investors from being able to make an objective decision as to the true value of the bank's shares.

The banks issued high-risk mortgages (sub-prime) and packaged them, by the previously described process of securitisation. The risky sub-prime debt was then transferred into Special Investment Vehicles and the banks sold off the shares in these companies. We need to know to whom those shares were sold.

Transferring Irish bank liabilities to the Irish taxpayers

How did the Irish banks get themselves into such an awful mess?

People initially became aware that the banks were in trouble when their share prices collapsed by up to 50 per cent during the summer of 2008. The banks told the government this was as a result of short selling by international hedge funds (who were betting on their belief that the shares were grossly overvalued and would go down).

THE BANKS – THEY GAMBLED AND LOST

The banks assured the government that if they banned short selling this would rectify the problem. So the government agreed to the banks' request and banned short selling of financial stocks. But the shares continued to fall. This proved it was not short selling that was causing investors to dump the shares. It was evident that there were more serious problems, which the Irish banks were not revealing. Depositors then began withdrawing their funds, so the banks next asked the government to guarantee depositors' funds, and in September 2008 the government agreed to do this.

The government initially said this was necessary as the previous depositor guarantee was deemed to be inadequate. But when the text of the guarantee was revealed it became apparent that this was not actually what had been done: the government guarantee had actually ended up being something entirely different.

The Irish government guarantee covered not only depositors' funds but also the entire debts of the banks, up to €485 billion. This represented more than twice Ireland's Gross Domestic Product.

At the time, the Irish National Treasury Management Agency said: 'On 29 September 2008, the government put in place a guarantee arrangement to safeguard all deposits (retail, commercial, institutional and interbank), covered bonds, senior debt and dated subordinated debt. Total liabilities covered under the scheme amount to approximately €485 billion.' Yes, that's four hundred and eighty-five thousand million euro: €485,000,000,000.

This figure was so large that most people found it difficult to comprehend, but they now knew that whatever it was that the banks had been up to was very serious indeed. Once people got over the initial shock, it suddenly began to dawn on them that if property developers, who had paid €84 million per acre for Dublin building land, financed by these banks, defaulted on their loans, the Irish taxpayer was going to be held directly liable. This was sheer, irresponsible madness on the part of the government, to have saddled the Irish taxpayers with liability for such a colossal amount.

Why should this have anything to do with the Irish taxpayers in the first place?

For the previous five years while the banks were making billions in profits and their senior executives raked in colossal bonuses, the Irish taxpayer gained no benefit; but the instant the banks' reckless loan decisions began to default the government decided to transfer the banks' liabilities to the Irish taxpayer. Most sensible, fair-minded people saw this as not only being totally unjust, but also putting the entire financial well-being of the country in jeopardy. Finance Minister Brian Lehinan said: 'It is designed to improve the liquidity of the banks, which have suffered enormous falls in share prices.' He also warned that any banking collapse would have catastrophic economic consequences and that his measures were designed to improve confidence in the Irish banking system.

The cynical amongst you would be forgiven for thinking that this transfer of liability for bank debts to the Irish taxpayers was actually designed to remove responsibility from the banks for the highly dangerous risk-taking they had engaged in over the previous five years.

This was the same dangerous risk-taking by which the banks had previously claimed they had earned billions in profits, when in actual fact they were simply storing risky debt off balance sheet and not really making any of those billions in profit at all.

So the huge bonuses paid to their senior management, based on profitability, should not have been paid in the first place.

In the three years between 2005 and 2007:

- Bank of Ireland chief executive, Brian Goggin, was paid €23 million.
- Anglo Irish Bank chief executive, David Drumm, was paid €21 million.
- AIB chief executive, Eugene Sheehy, was paid €11 million.

(These figures reflect the value of their stock option awards as they were valued at that point in time.)

But in spite of the major bailout intervention by the government, bank shares continued to fall. By December 2008, the shares had fallen by up to 95 per cent and were then worth less than half of what they were three months previously, when the government 'guarantee scheme' was introduced.

The banks still had no plausible explanation as to why this was happening, beyond pointless clichés like 'this is caused by external forces beyond our control'. People then began to say that the banks were definitely hiding something. Or could it be that the international investment community simply realised that if the Irish government was exposed to the banks for €485 billion and any of these banks defaulted, the Irish state had no possibility of covering that level of liability. Because at this stage the Irish government announced it was broke and needed to borrow €20 billion in 2009 simply to cover day-to-day spending.

As of 1 January 2009, the banks still had not revealed what the true situation was. The Irish taxpayers, who had been forced to bail them out, still had no idea what the true levels of bank debts were, nor whether or not these banks were capable of trading their way out of the situation.

Another reason the Irish bank shares continued to fall could be that international investors no longer trusted management at these banks, because as recently as July 2008 the banks were saying they had no problems and everything was OK.

In December 2008, Anglo Irish Bank chairman, Sean Fitzpatrick, was forced to resign when it was discovered he had obtained €84 million in 'secret loans'.

A spokesperson for Anglo Irish Bank commented that Fitzpatrick's decision to resign was 'based on the fact that, over a period of eight years to 2007, he temporarily transferred loans with Anglo Irish Bank to another bank prior to the group's year-end accounts. This transfer of loans did not breach banking or legal regulations. It was, however, inappropriate from a transparency point of view. It is important to state that the annual reports of the bank for each of the years in question represent a true and fair view of the bank. The disclosures in each of the annual reports were in full compliance with Companies Act requirements.'

This was a breathtaking illustration of a total denial of responsibility and of any acceptance by Anglo Irish Bank's management and board of directors that wrongdoing may have occurred.

On the Saturday after the government announced the €485-billion bank bailout, Fitzpatrick gave an interview on Marian Finucane's RTÉ radio talk show. When pressed, he thanked Irish taxpayers for the huge liability they had assumed for the banks' bad debts, but refused to say sorry for the crisis, adding that 'Irish banks were merely victims of the global credit crunch'. This represented yet another statement by a senior Irish bank executive illustrating dismissive arrogance and a complete denial of any personal responsibility for the reckless loan decisions which his bank had entered into. The Irish taxpayers were finding it increasingly difficult to put up with this sort of arrogance, especially as it was common knowledge that Anglo Irish Bank had milked the property bubble to the maximum. They became aggressive lenders, offering property developers and builders enormous loans which were speedily approved. These had now turned out to be bad loans, for development land and properties, which the bank should have known were grossly overvalued.

But in light of these facts, Anglo Irish Bank chairman Fitzpatrick was adamant that the Irish banks 'were merely victims of the global credit crunch'.

At this time, Sean Fitzpatrick was also under investigation by the Irish Stock Exchange.

Shortly after the banks had their initial meeting with the Minister of Finance to ask if the government would transfer liability for their bad debts to the Irish taxpayer and before the bank guarantee was announced, Sean Fitzpatrick purchased a very large amount of shares in Anglo Irish Bank and made a very significant profit from the deal. Fitzpatrick denied being guilty of 'insider trading'. Such a statement was also at odds with fiduciary duty: 'Breach of fiduciary duty may also occur in "insider trading", when an insider or a related party makes trades based on material, non-public, information obtained during the performance of the insider's duties at the company.'

Up to December 2008, while all this was going on, there was still no believable explanation being put forward as to what the banks had been up to, to cause such a catastrophic decline in their share values.

But around this time rumours were beginning to circulate about 'off-balance-sheet debts'.

Observers then began looking to the US and what had caused the huge investment bank Lehman Brothers to go broke. That's when the phrase 'mortgage securitisation' began to surface and people wondered if this had something to do with the crisis here in Ireland. In September 2008, when the government introduced the banking guarantee, they also instructed the accounting firm Price Waterhouse to have a look over the banks covered by the guarantee and report back to government by the end of November 2008. This report also seemed to cast no new light on the situation.

By this time, the Irish banks' ability to borrow funds internationally had all but dried up and it was beginning to look more and more like the banks were engaged in some sort of massive cover-up.

Of course, the real reason the banks were being shunned internationally was that they had an enormous amount of very bad loans on their books (or 'off their books' as it turned out), which were backed by underlying assets that carried bank valuations far greater than they were actually worth. These were the debts for which the Irish taxpayers had been compelled to accept liability.

It is bad enough being made liable for somebody else's debts, but to be made liable for debts that are known to be grossly overvalued was a particularly galling situation. Many Irish taxpayers were beginning to come to the conclusion that they were being taken for a ride by the banks, with the collusion of the government. Confidence in the government began to evaporate quickly and the question of political leadership, or the lack of it, was becoming a very real issue.

The boards of directors and senior management of the banks had presided over a 95 per cent collapse in their share prices and in so doing had destroyed the wealth of a whole generation of Irish people, who had invested their savings in these shares. The banks' reckless policies had also put private sector pension schemes at risk, as many of these were also invested in bank shares.

The bankers' behaviour could be deemed 'constructive fraud' as they engaged in acts, omissions and concealments that gave them an advantage over the investors. Even if such conduct was not actually fraudulent, dishonest or deceitful, there should still be legal grounds for redress by the investors.

By mid-December 2008, people began asking what was the Irish Financial Regulator doing, or not doing, while this economic catastrophe was unfolding. It then began to emerge that the Financial Regulator had been aware of the 'secret loans' that the chairman of Anglo Irish Bank had obtained, back in January 2008, and had not informed the Minister of Finance until the story broke in the Irish media in December 2008.

Or so the Minister said. But the Minister is a qualified lawyer and knows that 'ignorance is no defence'.

On 19 December 2008, the US President elect Barack Obama denounced American financial regulators for being 'asleep at the switch' as he laid the blame for the credit crisis and the world's biggest scam at their door. He added that both Wall Street regulators and congressional committees had failed the American people, who were frustrated that 'there's not a lot of adult supervision out there'.

Ireland – the only Eurozone country to guarantee bank debts

On 12 October 2008, we saw a Eurozone-wide agreement which increased the guarantees on customer bank deposits. Ireland, however, elected to opt out of such an arrangement 'given the 2008 Act had already ensured sufficient protection for our financial institutions'. The EU scheme also provided that 'Ministers for Finance would impose restrictions on guaranteed financial institutions, restrictions which must be notified to the European Commission', and also contained provisions 'to allow the Ministers for Finance to review the benefit of the guarantee obtained by any group companies of guaranteed banks to ensure the protection is not being availed of in a manner which is regarded as abusing the guarantee.'

THE BANKS – THEY GAMBLED AND LOST

November 2008: AIB, Bank of Ireland and Anglo Irish Bank each issued €2 billion in new bonds (commercial paper). Supported by the government guarantee, these bonds had the same quality as government bonds and quickly sold in the marketplace. What had the banks done with this money, which was raised on the back of the Irish taxpayer's guarantee? Irish business owners said they continued to be denied bank credit.

12 December 2008: AIB bank declined to comment on speculation that its Polish bank was interested in taking over AIG Bank Polska for around €350 million. Bank Zachodni WBK, in Poland, is 70 per cent owned by AIB bank.

One is reminded of the passage in the bank guarantee implemented by the other Eurozone members: '. . . to allow the Ministers for Finance to review the benefit of the guarantee obtained by any group companies of guaranteed banks to ensure the protection is not being availed of in a manner which is regarded as abusing the guarantee.'

Perhaps the Irish taxpayers would have been better served if their government had implemented the same guarantee scheme as the other Eurozone countries. If the banks' debts had not also been covered by the government guarantee then the bankers would have been forced to deal with the situation in a much more urgent fashion. As it was, the bankers were sitting pretty, the Irish taxpayers had been made liable for their debts and the issue was not now urgent as far as they were concerned and they could go back to seeing if they could figure out some new scheme for generating more large fees and extravagant personal bonuses.

The government seemed to have no idea what the banks were up to during this period.

One wonders if the banks were arrogant and reckless enough to continue securitising loans, after the government guarantee was put in place. Because the new 'securitised investment vehicles' would no longer need to be covered by Credit Default Swaps because the government was now the insurer.

Nobody really knows if this has happened because up to 1 January 2009 those same taxpayers, who had been made liable for the banks' previous recklessness, knew very little about what the banks were up to. The banks seem to have got carte blanche from the government to do whatever they liked, without any supervision or oversight of any kind. Beyond vague talk of appointing some other political pals to bank boards. The whole thing was absolutely disgraceful.

The Irish government's handling of the banks was beginning to make less and less sense. Any questions asked of the Finance Minister as to what was going on were repeatedly answered with bland, meaningless statements, such as: 'I have people looking into the situation and when they report back I will be in a better position to give you an answer.'

To most intelligent people, statements like this were translating into 'I don't have the faintest idea what's going on'. This was not the sort of leadership Ireland needed in its hour of crisis. The Finance Minister was being extravagantly paid to come up with solutions and he had none. The Taioseach was also bereft of ideas and the Tánaiste seemed to be totally bewildered by the whole situation. To be fair to them, none of the three had any experience in this field, so the question of competent leadership again arises.

In 2008, Eugene Sheehy, AIB Group Chief Executive, said: 'AIB delivered a strong performance in 2007. We are serving a growing number of customers in our high quality domestic and international franchises. The broad base and resilience of our business is a hallmark of AIB which positions us to deliver profitable growth in the more challenging operating environment for 2008.'

Also in 2008, Brian Goggin, Bank of Ireland Group Chief Executive, said: 'Bank of Ireland Group has delivered a satisfactory performance in difficult market conditions. Challenges and uncertainties remain, but looking ahead we are strongly positioned in our core markets and confident of our ability to maximise business opportunities, in an environment of moderating economic growth in the year ahead.'

On 22 October 2008, it was reported in the *Irish Independent* (in relation to the banks' bailout): 'Banking sources said that the tight window for institutions to sign up to the scheme was evidence the government was not open to negotiations on terms and conditions. It is being presented as a fait accompli.'

One wonders if the fait accompli was issued by the Irish government to the banks or by the banks to the Irish government.

By mid-December 2008, the banks were already looking for an extension to the government guarantee, beyond the initial two years. The banks said they were 'finding it difficult to raise loans for repayment beyond the guarantee date'. You can bet they were.

The banks were obviously now toying with the idea of parking liability for their debts with the Irish taxpayer on a more permanent basis. But by now the government's own massive borrowing requirement for 2009 was being affected by their massive exposure of €485 billion to the banks.

Other Eurozone governments announced that in 2009 they would be seeking to borrow large amounts from the international bond markets. Italy, France and Spain between them planned to raise €500 billion, while Greece and the Netherlands would be looking to raise more than €50 billion. Officials at Ireland's National Treasury Management Agency said: 'There were now possible difficulties of raising such funds while carrying the €485 billion exposure to the bank guarantee.'

In December 2008 German Finance Minister Peer Steinbrück accused the UK Prime Minister Gordon Brown of 'tossing around billions' and saddling a whole generation with a bill for paying off British debt. Steinbrück questioned whether Brown's £12.5-billion (€14.2-billion) cut in value-added tax would work. 'All this will do is raise Britain's debt to a level that will take a whole generation to work off,' he said, adding: 'The switch from decades of supply-side politics all the way to a crass Keynesianism is breathtaking.' One wonders what Steinbrück would have to say about the policies of the Irish government, which had exposed its taxpayers to liabilities of €485 billion?

Just how did the banks arrive at a situation where they ended up with grossly overvalued loan books? Because as we all know, most bankers are reasonably intelligent, bright people.

2004: With substantial increases in Irish property prices occurring every year, property developers and builders went on a house- and apartment-building spree, financed by the banks. The property bubble was getting up a head of steam. The builders and speculators were making ever-increasing profits, but not paying their workers correspondingly increased wages. But the construction workers and tradesmen were forced to look for higher wages as they were being priced out of the housing market as a direct result of the property speculators' enormous profit margins.

The Irish government of the day then decided to allow unlimited numbers of foreign workers into the country, which ensured a plentiful supply of cheap labour for the construction industry. This in turn affected the Irish workers' ability to get improved wages and, if they intended to buy a place to live, they were forced to borrow to feed the builders' and property speculators' ever-increasing profits. So Irish house buyers were forced into borrowing more and more money. The foreign workers spent very little of their earnings in Ireland and sent most of their money back to Poland, Lithuania, etc.

A bubble economy is born when wages trail productivity for a period of time, which in turn results in increasing levels of debt. This debt increases the amount of money in circulation and drives prices ever higher.

Eventually the Irish workers could no longer take on more debt to buy ever more expensive houses and apartments. That is when debt growth slowed down. This resulted in demand falling short of supply and suddenly Ireland had an over-supply of housing.

The normal reaction to this sort of situation would be for the banks to choke off credit to the builders and speculators and reduce the level of supply. But the banks continued lending and the excess supply of housing continued.

Next, bank share prices began to decline, because at this stage investors could see what was coming next and decided to bail out of the market.

Then Irish people began to default on the mortgages on their ridiculously overvalued houses, as they either became unemployed or their 'teaser mortgage rates' began to expire. That's when the banks' off-balance-sheet Special Investment Vehicles, which contained these mortgages, began to go into default because, when they were initially set up, they were sold on to unsuspecting investors as having guaranteed income streams for up to twenty-five years. That is when the party ended and the stock market crash in bank shares really hit. At this time a lot of the foreign construction workers began to return home, as work was drying up. The land speculators began to lock up their profits in bank deposits, under government guarantee, or invest them in overseas property, instead of putting these profits to productive use in the Irish economy. Irish banks are now owed almost as much by builders and land speculators (over €100 billion) as they are by mortgage holders.

Currently these property speculators and builders are reportedly being lent even more money by the banks to roll up interest on the loans. That way the banks do not have to classify the loans as 'out of order' and this allows them to be carried on the banks' loan book at full value. But many of these loans are probably worth about 50 per cent less than they were back in 2006–2007, particularly in Dublin city (where developers paid over €84 million an acre for building land). These are the loans which are now described as 'toxic debt,' and for which the Irish taxpayers have been made liable.

In December 2008, AIB head of retail banking, Donal Ford, told a Dáil committee: 'Prior to the EU's Basel II Directive, if a loan "went out of order" then it was between the borrower and the bank. But under Basel II it has to be categorised as a default . . ,' to ensure capital adequacy ratios remain in line.

Unless, you can find a way to 'hide' this debt. Enter mortgage securitisation and off-balance-sheet Special Investment Vehicles.

Bankers get millions in bonuses

Even the most unbiased observer would have to say there is something very wrong about a bank executive who pays himself €7 million a year while he runs that same bank into the ground and then expects the Irish taxpayers to accept liability for the all the 'toxic debts' he created. At the very least he should be compelled to return the millions he paid himself while he presided over the collapse of the bank and this should have been a pre-condition of any bailout.

If actions taken by the banks management during this period eventually led to billions in debts, the bank actually made no profits at all for the period. The bank executives who were granted their extravagant bonuses, based on profits, were not strictly entitled to them as the banks were actually making losses during the period and moving those debts 'off balance sheet' should not be allowed as a tactic to produce 'phony profitability'. One thing is glaringly obvious and that is that the banking leaders who got us into this mess are most certainly not the people qualified to get us out of it. Many years ago, former US Federal Reserve Chairman Greenspan said that he 'trusted the bankers to protect their own interests'. In 2008, he told a US Congressional Committee that he had 'made a terrible mistake in this assumption'.

At the beginning of this chapter I posed the question: 'Do the banks stand accused of knowingly providing 100 per cent mortgage debt to borrowers whom they must have known were going to default, especially as some of these loans were for several times the borrower's income?'

The answer has to be yes, because no one in the sub-prime mortgage market, from loan origination through securitisation, really cared about the risk of non-payment. Why? Because: (a) they got their fees paid up front; and (b) the risk was passed on – they sold it off. The greed for fees became a greed for bonuses as you moved up the ranks of mortgage brokers, stockbrokers and bankers.

- Over the past ten years, Irish house prices have increased about 300 per cent, compared to an increase of 30 per cent in the consumer price index.
- The average cost of a house in 1998 was €80,000. By 2007, this had increased to €300,000.
- Between 1998 & 2007, the average increase was 15 per cent per year.
- Commercial property usually follows residential downwards with a lag of about eighteen months.

Chapter 6

LOAN RANGERS – THE MORTGAGE
THREE-CARD TRICK EXPLAINED

Éamon de Valera insisted on maintaining Irish as the
national language of Ireland. A protectionist at heart, he
believed that language was a better defence against
attack than any physical border. Banking secrecy has an unlikely parallel in the way it uses language to keep its shareholders at arm's length. Peel away the terminology, however,
and you're left with a fairly simple tale of how greed, in the
way mortgages were managed in Ireland, led to an overheated economy and, ultimately, recession. Not unlike
Éamon de Valera, our bankers had a moral duty to protect
the interests of the people under their wing. Instead, they
abused the trust placed in them and used language to
obscure rather than illuminate their activities.

CELTIC MELTDOWN

What is mortgage securitisation?

It is the practice of converting illiquid (not easily sold) individual loans into saleable shares. This accelerated the speed at which banks could increase lending because it reduced the amount of capital needed for each new loan. It was widely adopted because of the way it ramped up returns on capital. But it is also a process that allows bankers to hide enormous debts 'off balance sheet' and make huge profits and bonuses in the process.

How was this done?

Banks traditionally operated by taking deposits from their customers, which they would then lend to people seeking loans. The difference between the interest rate paid on deposits and the higher interest charged on loans ('the spread') was their profit. If customers defaulted on their loans, banks were liable to depositors for payment and the banks held 100 per cent of the risk 'on their books', accepting complete responsibility. The borrower needed to have a good income, adequate assets, and make a generous down payment. This conservative approach to lending enabled banks to make healthy profits for decades and remain financially sound. This is known as the 'originate and hold' banking model.

Then, a few years ago the banks changed their traditional way of operating, as the huge growth in the mortgage market encouraged them to look for more 'creative' financing solutions. The banks decided to borrow money from people who were not depositors in order to issue more loans. They decided to raise this money by selling shares (or bonds).

In 2001, the Irish government passed the Asset Covered Securities Act 2001. This allowed for the setting up of non-bank mortgage finance companies. One wonders if the government who passed that legislation had any idea of what they were letting the country in for? Probably not. They 'trusted' the financiers who probably advised them this was 'required legislation for an orderly development of the Irish credit markets'.

But this piece of legislation was instrumental in infecting Ireland's financial system with the deadly sub-prime toxic-debts.

Mortgage securitisation

The reason it is called 'securitisation' is because 'securities' are (in the US, where this practice originated) another name for 'shares' and the investors were buying shares in the new companies, Special Investment Vehicles.

This was to be the foundation of the new Irish, 'originate and distribute,' banking model.

Under the 'originate and distribute' model, the banks would continue to make loans, but they would not hold onto them. They would package the loans into Special Investment Vehicles, backed by the anticipated cash flow from the portfolio of mortgages, and then sell these on to other financial institutions, such as pension funds. Many of these Irish 'securitised vehicles' contained mortgages with values running into billions. Once the securitised package was sold off, the banks could start the same lending process all over again.

In 2006, AIB and Bank of Ireland set up new 'off-balance-sheet' companies into which they intended to package Irish residential mortgages. Up to that point these two banks had issued bonds backed by Irish mortgages (all prime mortgages) to the value of about €7.5 billion. These two banks began this method of mortgage finance in 2004. In December 2006, Ulster bank put together a 'package' valued at €3.8 billion, which was one of the largest individual mortgage securitisations in Europe up to that time. So you can see, all this mortgage securitisation activity is very recent.

Then Ulster Bank subsidiary First Active put together a securitisation deal valued at €1.8 billion.

Others involved were EBS Building Society, which set up a number of new companies under the Emerald Mortgages brand name. Irish Life & Permanent were also active in this market and had set up a number of new 'Special Investment Vehicles' under the Fastnet Securities name. One of these Fastnet companies contained 13,121 mortgages valued at €2.15 billion. Irish Life & Permanent, similar to other companies, had asked the Irish Financial Regulator: 'that these companies should not be published on the Financial Regulator's website'. The Regulator obliged. One wonders if he fully realised what was really going on.

Irish banks were still creating more of these new off-balance-sheet companies as recently as November 2008. This would certainly seem to be an abuse of the government's guarantee scheme, because the Irish taxpayer was being made liable for yet more new bank debt long after the government stepped in to bail out these banks back in September 2008.

The sub-prime market

The Irish sub-prime market really began in April 2006 when Start Mortgages set up a €370-million securitisation deal, with an investment vehicle called 'Lansdowne Mortgage Securities No. 1'. This was quickly followed by a second deal, worth €525 million, 'Lansdowne Mortgage Securities No. 2'. These were backed by cash flows from a portfolio of sub-prime mortgages.

Start Mortgages was a specialist mortgage lender, established in 2004, under the Asset Covered Securities Act 2001, and was owned by UK specialist sub-prime mortgage provider, Kensington Mortgages. Kensington began its 'residential mortgage securities' business in 1996 and became the UK's largest provider of sub-prime mortgages.

Start operated only through brokers, from its headquarters in Clonskeagh, Dublin. It outsourced its mortgage administration to Home-Loan Management, based in Derry, Northern Ireland.

Start approached investors throughout Europe with its Irish offerings. As with others in the sub-prime market Start Mortgages paid the rating agencies to rate their investment packages. Initially, Barclays Capital arranged the finance, KPMG provided tax advice and McCann Fitzgerald were the legal advisers.

The Start mortgages were sub-prime (high risk) and, by the end of 2007, when these mortgages began to default and

Start began to initiate High Court repossession proceedings, Stepstone Mortgages, another sub-prime joint venture between IIB Bank (which was rebranded by its Dutch parent KBC in October 2008) and disgraced US bank Lehman Brothers, began refinancing these mortgages, provided the mortgage holder could demonstrate they could make three consecutive mortgage payments. Start repossession cases were dropped at the last minute because Stepstone had offered to refinance the debt. When questioned about the practice, Stepstone said: 'Offering to refinance mortgage debt to people is standard practice in the market. The company does not proactively seek or deal with customers directly; all business is generated via regulated brokers.'

Merrill Lynch had a similar sub-prime joint venture going with Irish Life & Permanent, called Springboard. In 2008, Lehman Brothers went bust and Merrill Lynch was taken over.

Dublin's International Financial Services Centre

Another benefit that Irish banks got from securitisation was that it dealt with complex tax issues which arise on large property finance transactions. The use of a 'Class X Note' became a feature of many Irish 'mortgage-backed investment vehicles'. This allowed for the stripping out of very large profits, as the paid-up principal on the note was limited to a nominal amount, usually about €50,000. Irish securitisation tax laws allow for a full tax deduction on interest paid on these notes.

The Dublin International Financial Services Centre (IFSC) also came in useful.

LOAN RANGERS

In January 2008, the Central Bank said: 'There was an unusually large increase in lending to non-bank IFSC companies during 2007. Some of the rise was accounted for by loans to Special Purpose Vehicles.' In December 2007, lending to non-bank IFSC companies increased by €1.1 billion during that month alone.

In the switch from 'originate and hold' to 'originate and distribute' banking, if a bank wanted to grant you a €150,000 mortgage, they did not need to get 100 new customers, each with €1,500 on deposit, to cover it. What some of them began doing was giving the loan at a rate of, say, 6.5 per cent, and then assume that they would be able to borrow the money on the open markets at a lower rate, of, say, 4.5 per cent. The 2 per cent difference would be enough to cover their costs and make a good profit.

Lenders generally tried to get customers to accept mortgages tied to LIBOR/EURIBOR rates, so if the rate the banks had to pay went up, the bank would earn more.

LIBOR and EURIBOR are interest rates at which banks lend money to each other. LIBOR/EURIBOR change constantly, but many customers wanted fixed-rate mortgages and this resulted in the banks becoming even more 'creative'. Some decided to take on the risk and try to forecast the changes in interest rates over a period of two to three years. Then they could price their fixed rates at a level which they believed would make a profit. Some decided to then 'hedge' that risk and they did this by buying an 'insurance policy', called a Credit Default Swap, a CDS.

Credit Default Swaps

By law a bank needs to keep large amounts of capital in reserve in case any of their loans go bad. But what if the bank could create a device that would protect it if those loans defaulted, and free up that capital?

So the banks came up with a sort of insurance policy: a third party would assume the risk of the debt going bad, and in exchange would receive regular payments from the bank, similar to insurance premiums. The bank would then get to remove the risk from its books and free up their reserves. This is what 'Credit Default Swaps (CDSs) were 'supposed' to do.

But the CDS market had no proper regulation and all contracts were privately negotiated so there was no transparency. This meant the system was wide open to abuse. Essentially, a CDS is insurance cover against failure of a risky investment. The important issue is, however, that this is not officially regulated as insurance. Credit Default Swaps are simply treated as contracts between two companies. Credit Default Swap companies would not guarantee any specific sum of money available to pay back any contracts. Insurance companies are required to do this. Many of the companies involved did not have the capital to pay out on their contracts, so when time came to call on the insurance guarantee, the money was not there. These companies were generating big returns selling these swaps with the appearance of taking on little risk, even though the losses could be immense if defaults actually did occur.

As we now know, defaults did occur and the whole house of cards began to fall.

Why did that happen?

CDS Co Ltd would tell AN Irish Bank that they could set up Credit Default Swap cover on a €5-billion package of sub-prime mortgages the bank was putting together. For this they would charge a sum of €5 million annually. The bank could now declare these mortgages as safe, because they were 'insured'. CDS Co Ltd made €5 million annually for doing nothing and in the process paid very generous salaries and bonuses to all executives involved. Then, when the bank's sub-prime mortgages begin to default, they said to their investors: 'That's not a problem, we are insured, so we'll recoup the losses'.

Next the bank calls on CDS Co Ltd to cover the losses and CDS Co Ltd says: 'Sorry, we don't have the money to cover you'. CDS Co Ltd then folds up, having operated for five years earning €5 million annually. But when CDS Co Ltd went out of business because of the bank's 'call' on the 'insurance' cover, the damage caused was far greater than just that deal, because CDS Co Ltd automatically defaulted on many other CDSs they had on their books: the damage is magnified and spreads out over a wide range of other investments.

If you questioned a banker as to the true nature of a Credit Default Swap you would more than likely be bamboozled with gibberish. The quality of the underlying asset (the original sub-prime mortgage loan) was the key. If that had been incorrectly valued (or overvalued as was normally the case) in the first place, failure was guaranteed.

Of course mortgage brokers cared little about the quality of the original loan, or the ability of the borrower to pay back, because they got paid their commission when they closed the original sale.

Neither were banks much bothered about the quality of the loan (as they illustrated by issuing 100 per cent mortgages for up to seven times a borrower's income on houses and apartments that were known to be grossly overvalued) because they intended to sell the loan off, by way of securitisation. The banks raked in huge profits and the bank executives and mortgage brokers skimmed off huge fees and the investors were landed with a mountain of what became known as toxic debt.

These same bankers who created this racket must have thought the Irish government was particularly gullible when they then agreed to make the Irish taxpayers liable for all these toxic debts.

All 'asset-backed investment vehicles' had similar characteristics:

- They had no history of financial returns.
- Banks told everyone that this was an exceptional investment. They talked about a 'Special Investment Vehicle' which was AAA rated and guaranteed by insurance cover through a Credit Default Swap (CDS). Although in many cases the AAA rating could not possibly be supported with even the most basic investigation of the underlying package of loans.
- The only people who collected on this investment were the mortgage brokers who got their fee immediately when they issued the original loan, and the bankers who

creamed off huge bonuses when these sub-prime loan packages were securitised and sold on.

• The method used by the bankers to skim off their huge bonuses was by way of another scheme called 'mark-to-market' (MTM). This allowed the bankers to draw down their bonuses in advance. This racket is known as 'front-loading the deal'.

MTM – Front-loading the deal

Mark-to-Market (MTM) works in the following way: if a bank issued a 25-year €400,000 mortgage, that mortgage would be worth, let's say, €750,000 to the bank over the 25-year life span of the loan.

The bank then immediately formed an 'Asset-backed Investment Vehicle', and sold the loan to the new company at its full 25-year value of €750,000. The bank then booked an immediate €350,000 profit on the deal and the banker skimmed off his 10 per cent bonus of €35,000.

Now if the 'Asset-backed Investment Vehicle' contained 1,000 mortgages, valued at €500 million, you can see where greed quickly came to the fore and banished all vestiges of probity.

An important characteristic of MTM is that it prevents an investor from assessing the true book value of a company engaging in this practice. If assets are carried at cost, the investor can analyse the market to see what the assets would be worth in liquidation, and thus calculate the risk associated with purchasing shares in a company based on its book value. When the company is permitted to front-load the value of its deals, investors lose a key reference point, cost, which is necessary to determine the true underlying value of the company.

Front-loading prevented the market price from being objectively determined. So the assets were being valued in a hypothetical manner using estimated valuations derived from 'financial modelling', which were subjective at best and possibly spurious.

Do you think the above practice is at odds with: 'A fiduciary is held to a standard of conduct and trust far greater than the comparable "duty of care" in common law. A fiduciary must avoid "self-dealing" or "conflicts of interests" in which the potential benefit to the fiduciary is in conflict with what is best for the person who trusts them. For example, a banker must consider the best investment for the client, and not buy or sell on the basis of what brings the highest commission for the banker.'

Marketing mortgages

Banks decided to outsource the sales process, and offered commissions to 'independent financial advisers' (mortgage brokers) who would sell their products.

Of course, if a mortgage broker's income is based on how many mortgages he or she sells, there is a tendency to become a bit lax in relation to qualification for the loan. This is what led to the term 'sub-prime mortgages'. In many cases, mortgage brokers, acting as agents for the banks, were economical with the information they gave to customers regarding terms and conditions, and the borrowers in turn provided the brokers with incorrect information. So we ended up with 'predatory lending' and 'predatory borrowing'.

The mortgage brokers were offering loans that had been originated by the banks. The banks in turn primed the pump and controlled production by financing the builders and developers, who were creating the feedstock for the mortgage loans. The banks financed the builders and land speculators, loaned the money for the mortgages and then securitised the loans. In reality, the banks were issuing home loans to people who really could not afford them, or under terms that virtually guaranteed that the borrowers would default. But the banks took a cut of each piece of the transaction, all the way up and down the line. They pushed mortgage brokers to stretch even their lax standards and issue risky loans on overpriced houses, the value of which could not possibly be supported with even the most basic investigation. Sometimes banks did not even bother to check the information provided.

'Predatory lending' was perfectly OK as long as it produced millions in bonuses for senior bank executives. When the bank securitised the loans and sold off shares in the new company, the bank would carry on doing the administration and charge the new company a fee for this. The income each month from the mortgage holders would belong to the new company and not the bank that extended the loan in the first place. That was how the loans went 'off balance sheet'. The new company usually paid a bit more than what was owed for the mortgages, allowing the bank to book an immediate profit. All this was good for the banks in many ways:

- They made an immediate profit.
- They got an ongoing valuable processing contract.
- They got someone else to take on the risk of borrowers defaulting.
- And most attractive of all, because the mortgages were 'not on their books,' the banks needed to keep less cash on deposit to comply with the 'capital adequacy' rules for lenders. The banks were then free to invest even more money in further 'toxic debt', for higher and higher fees and bonuses.

The new investors got to be mortgage lenders without all the administrative overhead of setting up processing departments, sales departments, etc. Plus, historically, most people really did pay their mortgages and it was therefore fairly easy to predict cash flow. Pension funds and other institutional investors, who know what their pay-outs are going to be each year, like to have predictable income. These new investors also had a 'liquid asset', in that they could now sell their shares in this new 'asset-backed investment vehicle' much quicker than they could ask for the repayment of a mortgage, if they needed cash in a hurry.

So to sum up, Special Investment Vehicles were limited liability companies set up by banks to shift debt 'off balance sheet' and to earn a profit by attracting funds from yield-seeking investors. The banks then used this money to structure yet more securitised deals or invest in financial instruments paying higher rates of return and higher fees. This sort of income vehicle was thought to be virtually risk-free because it had very high ratings from credit-rating agencies. But these same credit-rating agencies were being paid by the banks for the rating service.

For a few years, securitisation was a one-way street, and the fees and profits they generated added enormously to banks' profits and executives' bonuses. But eventually investors came to realise that the AAA-rated securities in which they had invested were little more than tarted-up bundles of overpriced and risky 'sub-prime' mortgages.

It was a highly profitable party while it lasted. But it was just a racket and, like all rackets, it finally folded. However, you can see why the 'originate and distribute' banking model was so attractive to the bankers.

Of course, all this was at the expense of lending to productive businesses which suffered as a result. In fact the 'ordinary' economy was reduced to existing on scraps from the banks. Why bother investing in manufacturing or service industries when you can make billions selling mortgages, bundling them into Special Investment Vehicles and flogging them to pension funds, which you probably control anyway? The more mortgages the banks could issue and bundle into Special Investment Vehicles, the more money they could make. To boost the trade, mortgage providers issued 'interest only' 100 per cent mortgages. They were able to justify this on the basis that six months after issuing the mortgage the house would be worth, say, 25 per cent more, which in turn effectively transformed the 100 per cent mortgage into a 75 per cent mortgage.

But it was destined to crash because it had been built on foundations of sand, created by the bankers. Everything went along fine while property prices kept on rising and Irish people continued to take on more and more debt. Until one day the hapless mortgage holders were no longer able to pay the mortgages on their grossly overvalued properties, because they became unemployed, or simply could not borrow any more. Then houses stopped selling and the whole house of cards began to crumble. Nobody wanted Special Investment Vehicles any more so the demand for ridiculously overpriced houses, apartments and development land vanished overnight.

The banks are now owed billions by developers and builders who have huge supplies of over-priced properties that nobody can afford. If nobody can afford them at their current prices, then they are deemed to be overvalued.

By how much are they overvalued? Anecdotal evidence would suggest by as much as 50 per cent. Which means the builders and developers can only sell these properties if they are marked down 50 per cent. But if they did that, the billions in bank loans to these people would have to be marked down 50 per cent. So time was running out for the Irish banks and, whichever way they cut it, the day of reckoning was drawing ever nearer. The 'toxic debt' on their loan books would have to be faced up to. It would have to be written down, or in many cases written off. But if the banks did that, they would be unprofitable for years to come and nobody would want to invest in their shares. At that stage, the banks, which had engaged in these practices, should have gone bust as would normally be the case with any business that had been run into the ground. As their credit problems mounted, banks sharply reduced lending to each other. None of the banks would disclose the true value of their 'dodgy debt' and trust between them evaporated. This then left the banks with no money to fund ordinary viable, commercial businesses. The 'credit crunch' had arrived.

The banks had one more throw of the dice left. They came up with a plan to save themselves from the predicament they had engineered. Get the Irish taxpayers to take on liability for all the banks' debts. But would the Irish government actually go along with this?

They did.

What is the exposure for the Irish taxpayer? €485 billion.

This was the same government who wanted old-age pensioners to forfeit their medical cards to save €70 million and the same government who also did not have €10 million to provide young Irish girls with a vaccine that would protect them from cervical cancer. Either our government was in cahoots with the banks or they were incredibly stupid. If anything goes wrong with the guarantee of the banks' debts, it is going to beggar Ireland's children, who will end up paying the consequences for years to come. The Irish taxpayers should definitely not become liable for these worthless debts.

Has the government's largesse improved the banks' position?

No.

Why?

Because the bank shares continued to fall even after the government guarantee was introduced.

Why the whole house of cards fell down

This process has been going on for the better part of twenty years without much incident. So, what went wrong now?

The biggest problem with securitisation is that no one has a vested interest in performing due diligence on the borrowers, the people taking out the mortgage loans. The mortgage brokers write the loan and sell it to a large investment bank. The investment bank pools the mortgage and carves it up into different bonds. Now, let's take your mortgage and pool it with other people who have similar mortgages (i.e. who pay a similar interest rate for a similar period of time). This would create a big pool of mortgages that pretty much had the same characteristics, meaning the first payments were composed of interest and the last payments were composed of principal with middle payments composed of a mixture of income and principal.

Now suppose you are a manager for an investment fund that invests entirely in bonds and you expect an increase in withdrawals in five years as fund investors retire. You need to figure out a way to raise cash in five years. It would be great, therefore, if you could buy a bond that guaranteed payment of principal and interest within your time frame. Suppose there are other fund managers in a similar position, who need cash that comes due within a specific time period. But their time period is different from yours. Some need the money now, some need the money in thirty years' time, etc. The problem, therefore, was how to combine the interests of the people paying the mortgage and the people who needed money at a certain time.

This is where collateralised debt obligations came into play. Instead of making one big pool of mortgages, we 'carve up the cash flows' – meaning we make a series of bonds that pay people at different times. This 'slicing and dicing' created what became known as collateralised debt obligations (CDOs). For example, one bond will pay principal and interest to a specific bond holder for three years and another bond holder will get principal and interest payments for ten years, etc. So you are pooling a group of mortgages with similar characteristics (interest rate, length of maturity) and directing the various cash flows to different people at different times. The bond holders do not hold all the collateral, only pieces of it. As a result, no one really owns all the mortgages for an extended period of time. Instead, the most they own is a piece of a larger pool of mortgages.

Now remember, we're using collateral composed of residential mortgages. What if we're writing a lot of mortgages to people who aren't creditworthy? That is the key to the current banking crisis, worldwide. Mortgage brokers wrote a lot of loans for people who could not afford them. In other words, the collateral used as the basis for the mortgage-backed bonds was bad collateral and no matter how you carve the cash flows, you are still using collateral that will eventually default.

That is what has been happening over the last few years. As loan defaults increased, the bonds backed by the collateral stopped paying interest and principal. That was the point at which banks, pension funds, hedge funds and anybody who invested in these collateralised debt obligations began to lose billions. This is at the core of the current crisis in the banking system. The repackaging of mortgages into residential mortgage-backed securities has fractured the ownership of the original mortgages and redistributed them so widely that the bank's and the government's hands are tied. To be able to modify the underlying mortgages one would need to own a substantial majority of the securitisation pools into which the mortgages have been transformed. That would be difficult, if not impossible, to achieve. And if it were possible, it would be exorbitantly expensive.

The Irish government is currently giving the banks billions of taxpayers' money just to keep them from going bankrupt for a little while longer. Because, unless the collateralised debt obligations can be unwound (which they can't), the underlying problem will still exist.

What does past experience say about the effectiveness of government intervention of this nature?

In Japan, the Nikkei stock market index hit a high of 39,957 in 1989, and then Japan's property and stock market bubble burst. The Nikkei index in the spring of 2009, twenty years later, is still trading below 7,600.

Even after twenty years of trying to turn its market around, Japan's numerous stimulus plans and near-zero per cent interest rates have not worked. Average annual growth remained at 1.5 per cent throughout the 1990s and in the last quarter of 2008 Japanese GDP contracted at an annual rate of 12.7 per cent.

Floating rate notes

In addition to the problems with securitisation the banks have another major problem: paying off billions of debt coming due. At issue are so-called 'floating-rate notes' – these are securities used heavily by banks to borrow money. A large amount of those notes, which typically mature in two years, will come due over the next year or so, at a time when the banks are struggling to raise fresh funds. That is going to force the banks to issue expensive new debt. With each passing day, it is beginning to look like no amount of money will save these banks and the Irish taxpayers would be as well served by making a pile of all the billions the government is pouring into them and setting fire to it. The whole thing is a total and unmitigated disaster.

Example:
AIB MORTGAGE BANK
Issue of €1,000,000,000 Floating Rate Mortgage Covered Securities due 2 October 2013
under the €15,000,000,000 Mortgage Covered Securities Programme
Issue Date: 2 October 2008
Maturity Date: 2 October 2013
1. Issuer: AIB Mortgage Bank
2. Series Number: 7
3. Specified Currency or Currencies: euro (€)
4. (a) Aggregate Nominal Amount of Securities:
                    (i) Series: €1,000,000,000
                    (ii) Tranche: €1,000,000,000

The banks will never have enough money to repay the astronomical debts they have racked up and the government should seriously reconsider its policy towards them, before it is too late.

But let us not forget, until the summer of 2008 very many Irish people were drunk on property prices. Every bar and restaurant one went into, property was the sole topic of conversation. We need to remember that many of us were willing accomplices in the orgy of greed. We will have plenty of time to reflect on these matters as the coming recession bites ever deeper.

However difficult the road ahead, we must learn from past mistakes if we are to avoid repeating them. The bankers who created this mess still claim today that they were committed to the 'highest ethical standards' and 'this is caused by external forces beyond our control'. Their absolute denial of any responsibility for what has happened is breathtaking. The banks' boards of directors and senior executives are directly and collectively responsible for the entire mess and the government should wake up to this fact.

Chapter 7

BROKEN TRUST – THE FACTS

There are some differences, depending on jurisdiction, as to the interpretation of the term Fiduciary Duty. What you get here is a generally accepted interpretation of what the term refers to. When somebody invests in bank shares, or relies on a banker's advice, they are placing complete trust and confidence in that banker. Does the banker then have a 'fiduciary obligation'?

Fiduciary duty is the highest standard of care in law. The word itself comes originally from the Latin *fides*, meaning faith, and *fiducia*, meaning trust.

Fiduciaries can include bankers, business advisers, real-estate agents, brokers, or anyone who undertakes to assist someone who places complete confidence and trust in that person or company. When a person acts for another in a fiduciary relationship, the law forbids the fiduciary from acting in any manner adverse or contrary to the interests of the client, or from acting for his or her own benefit in relation to the subject matter.

The duties of a fiduciary include 'loyalty and reasonable care of the assets within its custody'.

A fiduciary is expected to be extremely loyal to the person to whom they owe the duty (the 'principal'): they must not put their personal interests before the duty, and must not profit from their position as a fiduciary, unless the principal consents. The client is entitled to the best efforts of the fiduciary on his or her behalf and the fiduciary must exercise all of the skill, care and diligence at his or her disposal when acting on behalf of the client.

A person acting in a fiduciary capacity is required to make truthful and complete disclosures to those placing trust in him or her, and he or she is forbidden to obtain an unreasonable advantage at the latter's expense.

Best interest of the beneficiary must be primary

A fiduciary is held to a standard of conduct and trust far greater than the comparable 'duty of care' in common law. A fiduciary must avoid 'self-dealing' or 'conflicts of interests' in which the potential benefit to the fiduciary is in conflict with what is best for the person who trusts them.

For example, a banker must consider the best investment for the client, and not buy or sell investments on the basis of what brings the highest commission for the banker.

While a fiduciary and the beneficiary may join together in a purchase of property, the best interest of the beneficiary remains primary. All of the fiduciary's actions must be performed for the advantage of the client.

The term also embraces legal relationships such as those between broker and client.

A fiduciary relationship extends to every possible case in which one side places confidence in the other and such confidence is accepted; this causes dependence by one individual and influence by the other. The courts will stringently examine any transaction by which a dominant individual obtains any advantage or profit at the expense of the party under their influence. A transaction, in which 'undue influence of the fiduciary' can be established, is void.

When a bank provides expert advice on which a client relies, a bank has a fiduciary obligation. As adviser, it should at all times act in the best interests of the client. Full disclosure of all actual or potential conflicts is vital. A fiduciary must not have a conflict of interest.

A fiduciary will be held to account if proven to have acquired a profit, benefit or gain from the relationship by one of three means:

- In circumstances of conflict of interest and duty;
- In circumstances of conflict of duty and duty;
- Taking advantage of the fiduciary position.

Conflict of interest and duty: A fiduciary must not put themselves in a position where their interest and duty conflict. In other words, they must always serve the principal's interests, subjugating their own preference for those of the 'principal'. The fiduciary's state of mind is irrelevant; that is, it does not matter whether the fiduciary had any ill-intent or dishonesty in mind.

Conflict of duty and duty: A fiduciary's duty must not conflict with another fiduciary duty. Conflicts between one fiduciary duty and another can arise, for example, when an agent, such as a real-estate agent, represents more than one client and the interests of those clients conflict. Therefore, the conflict of duty-and-duty rule apply.

Taking advantage of the fiduciary position: A fiduciary must not profit from the fiduciary position. This includes any benefits or profits which, although unrelated to the fiduciary position, came about because of an opportunity that the fiduciary position afforded. It is unnecessary that the principal would have been unable to make the profit; if the fiduciary makes a profit, by virtue of their role as fiduciary for the principal, then the fiduciary must report the profit to the principal. If the principal consents then the fiduciary may keep the benefit. If this requirement is not met then the property is deemed to be held by the fiduciary on constructive trust for the principal.

Breaches of fiduciary duty

Conduct by a fiduciary may be deemed constructive fraud when it is based on acts, omissions or concealments considered fraudulent and that gives one an advantage against the other because such conduct, though not actually fraudulent, dishonest or deceitful, demands redress for reasons of public policy.

Breach of fiduciary duty may also occur in insider trading, when an insider or a related party makes trades based on material, non-public information obtained during the performance of the insider's duties at the company. Where a principal can establish both a fiduciary duty and a breach of that duty through violation of the above rules, the benefit gained by the fiduciary should be returned to the principal because it would be unconscionable to allow the fiduciary to retain the benefit by employing his or her strict common law legal rights. This will be the case, unless the fiduciary can show there was full disclosure of the conflict of interest or profit and that the principal fully accepted and freely consented to the fiduciary's course of action.

Bank executives have a fiduciary duty to their company.

Bank executives must act in the best interest of the company, act as trustee in regard of the assets of the company, be honest, divulge all conflicts of interest, and exercise skill. For example, a banker cannot lend money to somebody who is known to be unable to repay it, or would have been shown to be unable to pay it had the bank carried out even the most basic inquiries. If a bank did so they could be liable to having engaged in:

- fraud & deceit
- negligent misrepresentation
- civil conspiracy to commit fraud
- breach of fiduciary duty
- aiding and abetting breach of fiduciary duty
- gross negligence

- negligence
- civil conspiracy
- promissory estoppel (which prevents a party from acting in a certain way because the first party promised not to, and the second party relied on that promise and acted upon it).

Consider this information, and you be the judge of whether our banks have behaved ethically or if they have broken trust with their shareholders. It will also be interesting to see how the Office of the Financial Regulator, the Minister of Finance and the Department of Justice view this situation. How these agencies of government deal with this will be illustrative of where they see our financial services industry progressing from here. If they try to fudge the issue, or perhaps ignore it altogether, they will be sending a clear signal to the international investment community of what the Irish government views as acceptable behaviour in its financial services industry.

Chapter 8

ANGLO IRISH SHARE SUPPORT SCHEME – ENTERPRISE OF DECEPTION

In the summer of 2009 ten customers of Anglo Irish Bank were lent €451 million to buy shares in the firm. The operation to buy 10 per cent of the bank was funded by borrowings from Anglo Irish itself and organised by then chairman Sean Fitzpatrick. The bank had loaned money to individuals who in turn were to buy the bank's own shares and thereby prop up their value by creating the impression that there was actual demand for the shares.

This was a very obvious illegal share support scheme. Section 60 of the Companies Act bars businesses from providing loans to third parties to buy their shares. In the most fundamental sense, such an operation aims at the creation of a false market. This was a cynical disregard of laws and regulations, a fraudulent misuse of bank monies and total contempt for truth and common honesty.

But this was not the first time that a major Irish company had been involved in an illegal share support scheme: over twenty years previously, in December 1986, a formal investigation of the Guinness company was opened by the UK Department of Trade & Industry (DTI). The Guinness case was the first major enquiry launched by the UK Serious Fraud Office.

The case involved an attempt to manipulate the stock market to inflate the price of Guinness shares and thereby assist a £2.7-billion takeover bid for a Scottish drinks company. From early 1986, Guinness plc had been engaged in a closely fought competition with Argyll plc to take over The Distillers Company plc. Their respective offers for Distillers included a substantial share exchange element and accordingly, their respective share prices were a critical factor for both sides.

In November 1986, amid rumours of misconduct during the course of the bid, the Secretary of State for Trade and Industry appointed Inspectors under the Companies Act 1985 to investigate the affairs of Guinness. The investigation involved:

1. Ernest Saunders, Guinness chief executive.
2. Sir Jack Lyons, a management consultant renowned for his philanthropy, whose acquaintances included former UK Prime Minister Sir Edward Heath.
3. Gerald Ronson, property tycoon, head of the Heron empire and the man credited with bringing self-service petrol stations to Britain.
4. Anthony Parnes, a trader on the London Stock Exchange.

By 1990, fraud investigators had amassed sufficient evidence to bring all four to court.

The DTI said that Saunders, while not the author of the share support operation, had been fully aware of its progress.

Unlawful share support

During the course of the takeover bid, the Guinness share price quoted on the stock market rose dramatically. It transpired that this was a result of an unlawful share support operation, which involved 'supporters' buying shares who were paid substantial sums from Guinness' own funds but without board authority – in effect the supporters were given secret indemnities against losses and, in some cases, equally secret and very large success fees. The indemnities and success fees were paid under cover of false invoices.

Ernest Saunders, the chief executive of Guinness at the time of the bid, was the only defendant who gave evidence at the trial.

At trial and in his evidence to the Department of Trade and Industry inspectors, he denied all knowledge of, or involvement in, the share support operation or the false invoices.

In the mid-1980s, at the height of the Thatcherite era, Saunders was heralded as one of the City of London's shrewdest deal-makers on the corporate scene.

To win Distillers and its top whisky brands Guinness had needed to make sure its shares were worth more than those of its rival Argyll and did so by recruiting wealthy investors to buy shares and cover any losses. Saunders was supported by the cream of the City of London establishment during the Distillers bid. Gerald Ronson was one of the supporters. His companies purchased approximately £25 million-worth of Guinness shares against the promise given by Saunders of an indemnity and a success fee of £5 million. False invoices, which bore no suggestion that they related to indemnities and success fees, were rendered to Guinness and paid. Ronson had told the DTI Inspectors that at the time, he did not think there was anything wrong with what he was doing, and he had trusted Anthony Parnes who had elicited Ronson's support. When interviewed by the Inspectors, Ronson was unable to explain why he thought Guinness should pay him £5 million to do something, which if it had been lawful, Guinness could have done itself.

Anthony Parnes had recruited Ronson as a supporter. After the bid, Parnes received a success fee of £3.35 million, negotiated on his behalf by Sir Jack Lyons, after he supplied a false invoice. Two further false invoices were submitted to Guinness and paid in respect of support recruited by Parnes from Ephraim Margulies, chairman of S & W Beresford plc. Parnes' defence at trial was that he had not acted dishonestly.

Sir Jack Lyons not only provided support himself but also recruited other supporters. He received from Guinness, under cover of false invoices, indemnity and success fees. Lyons denied to the DTI Inspectors that he had been involved in obtaining supporters or in drafting the false invoices. Lyons He claimed that if he had been approached to do this, he would have walked away.

All four defendants were convicted:

ANGLO IRISH SHARE SUPPORT SCHEME

Chief executive Saunders was found guilty on eight counts of false accounting, two counts of theft, and of conspiracy.

Sir Jack Lyons, aged 84, only escaped jail because of ill health and age, was fined £4 million for theft and false accounting and stripped of his knighthood.

Anthony Parnes was jailed for two and a half years for false accounting and theft.

Gerald Ronson was jailed for a year and fined £5 million.

Ronson, Parnes and Lyons were all ordered to pay £440,000 in costs. Saunders' five-year sentence was halved on appeal and he was released from open prison after serving only ten months.

Chapter 9

SWEDEN'S BANKING MODEL – WOULD IT WORK IN IRELAND?

The Irish government has employed economist Peter Bacon 'to assess the possibility of creating a "bad bank" or risk insurance scheme to take so-called "toxic debts" off the banks' balance sheets in a bid to free up new lending'.

The banks, naturally, think this is a great idea and say that it was very successful in Sweden.

But Sweden's banking crisis was not the same as Ireland's. The Swedish banking system in 1992 was in deep trouble. After years of very lax regulation, short-sighted economic policy and the end of a property boom, its banking system was, for all practical purposes, insolvent. The story sounds very familiar so far.

Interest of rates of 500 per cent

Financial deregulation in the 1980s caused a frenzy of real-estate lending by Sweden's banks and they did not worry about whether the value of their collateral might evaporate in tougher times. The bubble deflated fast in 1991 and 1992 and property prices imploded. A vain effort to defend Sweden's currency, the krona, caused overnight interest rates to spike at one point to 500 per cent.

The Swedish economy contracted for two consecutive years after the long expansion, and unemployment, at 3 per cent in 1990, went to 12 per cent by 1993.

The first big bank to collapse, Nordbanken, was already government-owned and had been for years. So when it failed it was not an issue of the government taking over a private company, it was a bank being rescued by its biggest shareholder, which happened to be the government. Only one other bank was nationalised, Gota Banka, a relatively small one. The government also created a so-called 'bad bank' to take on troubled assets, mostly real estate, which was sold off once market conditions improved.

Up until the crisis of the early 1990s, Sweden's government was not very good at managing a bank. In fact, the government's bad management *caused* the crisis to begin with. However, after the mid-1990s and right through to the present day, the Swedish government has done an excellent job with Nordbanken's successor, Nordea.

But Sweden did not just bail out its financial institutions by *solely* having the government take over the bad debts: it got commitments from bank shareholders before any bailout.

Sweden told its banks to write down their losses promptly, *before* going to the state for recapitalisation. So the banks had to write down drastically the overpriced property assets they had been carrying on their loan books and issue warrants to the government. That strategy held banks responsible and turned the government into an owner.

The Irish government has not compelled the Irish banks to do this.

Sweden decided to guarantee all the liabilities and the depositors while at the same time, in those banks where there was no value left, they let the shareholders be wiped out through nationalisation.

The decision to not protect the bank's owners mobilised public support for using huge amounts of taxpayers' money for rescuing the banking sector. The Swedish government insisted that for every krona they put into banks they got shares in return. That ensured they did not have to go into certain banks at all.

By the end of the crisis, the Swedish government had seized a vast portion of the banking sector, and the new agency had mostly fulfilled its very strict mandate to drain share capital before injecting cash. When markets stabilised, the Swedish state then reaped the benefits by taking the banks public again and more money may yet come into official coffers. The government still owns 20 per cent of Nordea, a Stockholm bank that was fully nationalised and is now a highly regarded giant in Scandinavia and the Baltic Sea region.

Before giving any bank new capital, the Swedish government conducted a detailed examination of the banks' records to see if they were still solvent (something else the Irish government has not done). It recapitalised the solvent banks in exchange for government equity, and fully nationalised the two banks that were not solvent, in both cases allowing highly qualified inspectors to oversee those banks operational policies. By intervening so forcefully, it spurred banks that did not want to be partly government-owned and closely monitored to move fast to fix their problems by raising new private capital on their own.

The politics of Sweden's crisis management were similarly tough-minded, though much quieter. Soon after the plan was announced, the Swedish government found that international confidence returned more quickly than expected, easing pressure on its currency and bringing money back into the country. The centre-left opposition, while wary that the government might yet let the banks off the hook, made its points about penalising shareholders privately and the government ensured this was done.

When distressed assets were sold, the profits flowed to taxpayers, and the government was able to recoup more money later by selling its shares in the companies as well.

Sweden spent 4 per cent of its gross domestic product (GDP), the equivalent of $11.7 billion at the time, or $18.3 billion (approx. €13.25 billion) in today's money, to rescue the ailing banks. But the final cost to Sweden ended up being less than 2 per cent of its GDP. Some officials say they believe it was closer to zero, depending on how certain rates of return are calculated.

Sweden emerged with a healthier financial sector that has withstood the shocks of the current global meltdown relatively well.

Goran Lind, a Swedish central bank official involved in the bailout, said afterwards: 'To get out of a crisis you have to restore confidence towards the banks. All involved must trust that the full scope of the problem has been disclosed and that there is a credible solution. That's what permeated our thinking in the '90s.'

That is what is missing in Ireland: the banks will not open up their books and disclose what the real problems are, or how big they are.

Sweden bailed out its banks with €13.25 billion in today's money, the Irish banks have had to get a government guarantee of €485 billion, indicating that Ireland's problem is vastly bigger than the one Sweden faced.

There are other reasons why the Swedish model will not work here.

A large part of the Irish bank's 'toxic debts' are property-related mortgages, the vast majority of which were securitised, and the government cannot purchase mortgages directly out of securitisation pools.

The securitisation of mortgages into mortgage-backed securities, and their further slicing up into collateralised debt obligations (CDOs), have fractured the ownership of the original mortgages and redistributed them so widely that the government's hands are tied in that regard.

Also, the banks are still holding a portion of these securities, which they created, on their books. It is when these securities ran into trouble that the banking system itself was put at risk; because these are an unknown all banks then lost confidence in one another and the interbank lending market froze.

That is when we ended up with a full-blown financial crisis.

SWEDEN'S BANKING MODEL

In an interview with the UK *Guardian* newspaper in October 2008, Bo Lündgren, Director General of Sweden's national debt office, the country's financial regulator and Sweden's Finance Minister in the early 1990s, said US proposals to cap bankers' pay as part of their bailout did not go far enough. He said laws should be introduced in Europe, making it a criminal offence for bankers to lend irresponsibly. He also proposed that banks should be made subject to legally-binding guidelines on lending.

He said legislation should be introduced so that bank executives responsible for reckless lending would be punished under criminal law, or be forced to pay damages. He criticised Ireland's decision to offer a 100 per cent guarantee to protect deposits and debts. 'I was astonished by what the Irish government has done,' he said. 'This distorts competition and the integration of capital markets across Europe. If one country in Europe offers a blanket guarantee, it puts pressure on everyone else to do the same.'

He said the EU should not follow the US example of buying up banks' toxic assets without taking stakes in them. 'You will never win an election for measures to support banks, but taking stakes in banks would be more popular. This is because taxpayers stand to gain in the future if the banks' share prices rise.'

Chapter 10

LET FAILED BANKS FAIL – WHY NOT?

The Irish bankers who created this economic crisis which has brought our economy to its knees have walked away with millions, without an admission of guilt, an explanation, or an apology.

These same bankers are now looking for rule changes that will allow them to avoid biting the bullet and making the real decisions that will end this crisis, namely, writing down or writing off the huge amount of ridiculously overpriced assets they have built up in their loan books, otherwise known as toxic debt. These bankers tell us that the normal rules of the game should be forgone when markets 'stop functioning properly'.

What statements like that really mean is that the bankers used these rules to pay themselves millions and in the process destroyed their banks and they now want these rules suspended so they can continue to carry on doing the same thing.

LET FAILED BANKS FAIL – WHY NOT?

Our bankers are constantly looking for ways to make their companies' financial statements reflect the 'management's assumptions'. But as long as banks are allowed to continue denying the true value of these toxic assets, the longer the current financial impasse will continue.

But, of course, if these banks are all of a sudden forced to own up to the reality of their huge losses, their balance sheets will show the true nature of the catastrophe they have created. There is no point in trying to hide this any longer: people now know what has happened and it will not go away. The government would be very foolish to think that they can continue playing these games with the bankers, because the Irish taxpayers will stand only for so much of this kind of carry-on.

Any attempt by the government to set up a 'bad bank' to transfer ownership of the bankers' toxic debt to the Irish taxpayers will simply mean that the heroin addict is being allowed to call the shots, because rehabilitation will hurt more than continued dysfunction and the prospects for finally breaking the impasse are kicked farther down the road. It is just another barefaced attempt to have the bankers win again, at the expense of the Irish taxpayers.

The main problem with the banks is not a lack of liquidity. If it were, then the government could simply provide them with funds without loan guarantees. The real issue is that the banks made bad loans in a bubble and were highly leveraged. They have lost their capital, and this capital has to be replaced.

Paying fair market values for the assets will not work. Only by overpaying for the assets will the banks be adequately recapitalised. But overpaying for the assets simply shifts the losses to the Irish taxpayers. In other words, the 'bad bank' plan only works if and when the Irish taxpayer loses big time.

It is high time the government accepted reality here and allow these failed banks to go into bankruptcy.

Back in September 2008, when the shares in major Irish banks began to fall, the bank's senior executives told the government that this was caused by international short-sellers (people who were placing bets which were forcing the shares down) and they asked the government to ban short selling of their shares, which the government did. The ban became effective from midnight on 17 September 2008.

On 19 September 2008, Bank of Ireland closed up 38 per cent per cent to €5.20. Anglo Irish Bank advanced by 28.7 per cent to €5.60. AIB increased 19.4 per cent to €6.23.

Now, the more cynical amongst you could be forgiven for thinking that maybe this jump in prices was as a result of the bankers buying each other's shares. Whatever the reason, it was short lived and within days the shares were falling again.

Example: Bank of Ireland share prices (Bank of Ireland).

The shares continued to fall, because the real reason Irish banks were under pressure was that they were carrying billions of bad property-related loans on their books. The banks did not want to admit this and tried to camouflage their own reckless lending behaviour by blaming short-selling speculators.

Next, the banks went back to the government again, saying that depositors were taking money out of the banks and their new story was that this was a result of scare programmes on the radio.

So the government again believed the banks and on 19 September decided to issue a guarantee on all depositors' funds. The Finance Minister Brian Lenihan said: 'deposits are not now in any danger and people should not be going to banks to shift their deposit accounts on the basis of unfounded allegations made on radio programmes.'

Bank guarantee shock

The full details of the government bank guarantee were not released until a month later, on 15 October 2008, and it revealed something far different from a guarantee covering depositors' funds.

Under the scheme, Irish taxpayers had been made liable for debts in all the major banks, up to a mind-blowing €485 billion. The banks covered were AIB, Bank of Ireland, Anglo Irish Bank, Irish Life & Permanent, EBS Building Society and Irish Nationwide.

Game, set and match to the banks.

The Central Bank said the decision was taken to protect financial stability and to enable financial institutions to access funds and to provide credit to companies and households (which has not happened).

The Department of Finance said the step was being taken to remove any uncertainty surrounding banks and that it was a very important initiative by the government, designed to safeguard the Irish financial system. 'The Government's objective in taking this decisive action is to maintain financial stability for the benefit of depositors and businesses and is in the best interests of the Irish economy,' they said. 'This very important initiative by the Government is designed to safeguard the Irish financial system and to remedy a serious disturbance in the economy caused by the recent turmoil in the international financial markets,' the statement concluded.

So, according to the government, the whole episode was the result of 'the recent turmoil in the international financial markets' and had nothing to do with the Irish banks' reckless lending in bringing their companies to ruin and destroying the wealth of their shareholders.

Minister Brian Lenihan warned that any banking collapse would have catastrophic economic consequences for the state and he went on to say that one of the key provisions contained in the guarantee bill would be measures to prevent abuse of the scheme and a new committee would oversee bonuses and pay of directors and executives.

But, on 4 March 2009, the government defeated an opposition motion to cap bankers' pay and at the end of March 2009 the same minister, Brian Lenihan, said he had no control over bankers' pay and bonuses. The bankers had really pulled the wool over the government's eyes and were now free to go off and borrow more money in the international markets without any accountability to the Irish taxpayers who bailed them out.

Then, on 21 December 2008, the government agreed to give AIB €2 billion in funding and the bank was to raise government-underwritten equity of €1 billion. But, in spite of the government guarantee, AIB failed to raise the €1 billion. AIB's explanation for this failure was: 'This factor has been exacerbated by negative market sentiment following developments in the UK banking sector and the nationalisation of Anglo Irish Bank.' AIB might have been pulling the wool over the Irish government's eyes, but international investors were not so easily fooled. They were well aware that AIB had too much debt and very few sound assets.

Back in 2006, AIB had sold off their branch network, including their headquarters in Dublin, on sale and lease-back deals. In March 2009, AIB chief executive Eugene Sheehy said that between thirty and forty big names accounted for half the bank's €10.8 billion-worth of outstanding property development loans. He said they were working on the assumption that the bank will write off between €5.95 billion and €6.45 billion of bad loans, mainly as residential development loans turn sour, but warned loan losses could reach €8.5 billion.

If bank debts were this low, why did they require a government guarantee of €485 billion? Could it be that this was another false and misleading statement from an Irish banker perhaps?

Also at this time, credit rating agency Moody's downgraded AIB's long-term credit rating, saying the move was due to expectations that its bad debts would increase substantially.

But, not to worry, the Irish government was still a soft touch and it next agreed to give AIB and Bank of Ireland €3.5 billion each of Irish taxpayer's money.

Eugene Sheehy said: 'I welcome this initiative and consider that it strongly supports the vital objective of improving market confidence in Ireland, our banking system and AIB. I thank the Government for the positive and commercial approach taken in reaching this agreement.'

I bet he did. You will notice he never thanked the Irish taxpayers who gave the government the bailout money.

Around this time, AIB also admitted that Irish zoned land could fall in value by 70 per cent; unzoned land, 80 per cent; zoned land with planning permission, 70 per cent; and existing office, retail and industrial buildings could halve in value. It is no wonder the Irish banks support the idea of a government-created 'bad bank' which would buy up all their illiquid, rancid, junk debt.

Why the government was shovelling billions into these imploding banks was a complete mystery.

In March 2009, Eugene Sheehy said that he 'regretted some of the lending decisions that [his] bank, AIB, made in recent years and that the company could have made better decisions'.

So finally a bank was willing to admit, partially, that it was its own reckless lending practices and not 'international market instability' which were to blame for the catastrophic destruction of wealth that had occurred at the bank. You will notice of course that Eugene Sheehy blamed 'the bank' and not himself as chief executive for having made the 'bad decisions'.

Between 2004 and 2008 while this disaster was happening, and while Eugene Sheehy was in charge, he had paid himself €5.6 million, including bonuses of €2.15 million and conditional share awards, which were worth €6.8 million at the time they were granted. In the same period, Brian Goggin of Bank of Ireland paid himself €23.5 million, and David Drumm of Anglo Irish paid himself €21.4 million.

In March 2009, despite AIB's share price being almost wiped out, Sheehy said he had no intention of quitting his post. 'I see myself as being an experienced banker who wants to work through this cycle,' he said. I wonder how the shareholders, who had watched Sheehy preside over the destruction of their investments, felt about that little quip.

Reality check

In March 2009, the Irish government decided to give Bank of Ireland and Allied Irish Banks €7 billion of taxpayer's money.

In March 2009, you could have bought all the shares in the two banks for €1.25 billion.

In addition to this taxpayers' handout, the Irish retail clearing banks tapped the European Central Bank (ECB) for a record €29.5 billion in February 2009. So between February and March the Irish banks got cash bailouts from those two sources of €36.5 billion. In addition, in January Anglo Irish Bank (they haven't gone away, you know) raised €10 billion through an Asset Covered Securities Programme.

What have these banks been doing with these huge amounts of money?

We, the taxpayers, have no idea. But these failed banks could not raise one penny if it was not for the Irish taxpayers guaranteeing their debts. There is something terribly wrong with what is happening in the Irish banking community and our Minister for Finance seems to be selling the Irish taxpayers down the river. The taxpayers' guarantee on bank debts should be removed immediately, just as quickly as it was introduced. Then the three banks – AIB, BOI and Irish Life – should be allowed to fail immediately.

The shareholders will be wiped out, but the banks' senior management have already destroyed that wealth. The bondholders will also be wiped out, but they knew the risks they were taking when they invested in these 'zombie' banks. These failed entities are destroying, with each passing day, our borrowing capacity with the ECB without any accountability whatsoever as to what they are doing with the money. The Irish taxpayers are responsible for most of the capital the banks have today, yet the taxpayers have no control over how these banks are run.

The government could very easily have said 'not one penny of taxpayers' bailout funds are to go towards executive salaries and bonuses without first being cleared by the Finance Minister'. But the government did not do that, because it is weak and ineffective.

This government has done tremendous damage to the Irish economy in the way it has handled this crisis. If a new Irish bank had access to the €36.5 billion that these failed banks have got their hands on, it could immediately extend credit to 'productive' Irish businesses. Such a new bank, free of 'toxic debt' could leverage this capital of €36.5 billion by a factor of six, to give it reserves of €219 billion. This new bank would then be in a position to bail out the Irish residential mortgage holders, who are much more deserving of bailout than the bankers who created this entire mess.

Debt reduction

We must reduce the face value of home-owner debt. This would be the quickest way to restart the economy. It would put money directly into householders' pockets and would immediately boost consumption.

Current estimates put outstanding Irish residential mortgage debt at about €120 billion.

Most of these mortgages are held by AIB, BOI and Irish Life. By letting them fail, the new bank could pick up their housing assets for 50c on the euro, costing about €60 billion, reduce the value of these mortgages by the 50 per cent they had acquired them for and then refinance them with long-term mortgages that their owners can afford to pay. This could replace the current government mortgage-interest tax relief scheme and would not cost the government very much in real terms, but it would make a dramatic difference to the amount of disposable income available to Irish consumers each week. Just one quick fix, and that's it: bankrupt banks go bankrupt; Irish householders are bolstered back into consumption mode. Housing becomes more affordable and a floor is finally put under house prices. It would stabilise the property market and stabilise the debt associated with that market.

The new bank could also take over the failed housing schemes and apartment blocks at 50c on the euro (or less) and put them on the market at realistic prices (50 per cent less than they are currently offered at), with affordable thirty-year fixed-rate mortgages attached. This would resolve the predicament of nonperforming assets, remove the overhang of unsold housing and thereby start to breathe some life into the construction sector. Most importantly of all, it would make housing once again affordable for Ireland's young people and maybe prevent them from emigrating. Because the country desperately needs them to stay at home and help rebuild the country.

It should also be possible for the government to pick up the mortgage payments for the unemployed temporarily. This would dramatically reduce the social impact of unemployment and if the horror of the possibility of losing the family home is removed, that person could then be compelled to participate in a government employment scheme paying €400 per week instead of €204 dole per week for doing nothing. Most importantly of all, such a scheme would help that person maintain their dignity and be useful to society, rather than being a burden on it.

Investments like this have the capacity to bring huge returns to the government. It makes a lot more sense than increasing taxation and dribbling dole out to half a million people.

If you increase taxes on an already sharply declining economy, you don't have to be an economist to realise what effect that will have on the economic activity still remaining.

Increasing taxation when consumption is collapsing is a catastrophic mistake. When our economy is in trouble we need to stimulate demand, not choke it off. One of the major lessons from Japan was that, in 1997 when their economy was beginning to recover, they raised taxes because they wanted to get rid of their deficit, and the economy immediately sank back down into recession again.

Bad debt is the root cause of the crisis. So the crisis will not end until the issue is resolved. The major Irish banks have such a mountain of toxic debt that they will never be solvent, so they can never deal with the consumer debt issue and must be eliminated before they cause any more economic destruction. These banks have already destroyed their shareholders' wealth and will destroy the Irish economy if they are allowed.

On 2 April 2009, immediately after the government gave AIB and BOI €7 billion, Ireland's three biggest stockbrokers NCB, Davy and Goodbody said the government will have to put more taxpayers' money into the banks because they face losses of €25 billion owing to the collapse in the property market. I can assure you that €25 billion would not scratch the surface of the Irish banks' debts.

There is currently a €485-billion bank guarantee in place to cover these debts and if any major portion of that gets called in the country will be in ruin. Does it not make a lot more sense to spend €60 billion to reduce all residential owner-occupier mortgages in the country by 50 per cent as a means of jump-starting our economy and eliminating the massive burden of debt the Irish people currently find themselves saddled with?

All this debt reduction should start at the bottom and work its way up through the price levels, so that the millionaires would be last to be bailed out, and anybody qualifying for relief would have to demonstrate that they had the ability to finance the new, reduced mortgage.

Letting banks fail

The notion of letting banks fail is unthinkable to many people. Not so to some bankers and economists. They say bank failures, even large ones, do not necessarily hurt, and may even help, the economy. They say the end result will be a stronger, healthier banking system. This does not mean, however, that economists are unconcerned about the banking system: they are. But there are levels of concern and there are disagreements about it.

Some say the very big banks should be saved, but others say those, too, should be allowed to go down in the flames of their own excesses. They all agree that the banking system itself must be preserved. Only the banks, they say, can really be in a position to keep the engines of the nation's economy working: almost all Irish households and most of its businesses use banks to borrow money and, through current accounts, to pay for what they buy. Without such credit and smooth flow of payments, the economy quickly halts.

But there is no evidence that the Irish banking system is in any danger of collapse, mainly because in Ireland we have plenty of choice between banks, building societies, credit unions and Postbank. Because of the new options open to consumers, the major banks are not as important as they once were.

LET FAILED BANKS FAIL – WHY NOT?

Although most commentators find no evidence that the banking system is in any danger of collapse, virtually all agree that there are serious problems with some of the bigger banks, which must be urgently addressed.

The failure of a bank is no different from the failure of any other business; as long as the Central Bank keeps the overall quantity of money from declining, a bank failure will have no greater effect on the economy than the failure of any other commercial enterprise. In the past, the failure of a large bank created the risk that large, uninsured deposits, especially money from other banks, would be lost, causing the other banks to fail. But the Irish government's depositor guarantee scheme has overcome that problem.

Even if large depositors begin to pull out of a big – but weakening – bank, they will still put that money into some other bank. The money stays in the banking system; it is simply redistributed from risky to safe banks.

However, the decision to provide unlimited government protection for deposits at failed banks creates perverse incentives for depositors to keep their money in risky institutions, ultimately increasing the likelihood of bank failures.

Nobel Laureate and former chief economist at the World Bank, Professor Joseph Stiglitz of Columbia University says:

> Governments should allow every distressed bank to go bankrupt and set up a fresh banking system under temporary state control rather than cripple the country by propping up a corrupt edifice. There is a sound argument for letting the banks go bust. It may cause

turmoil, but it will be a cheaper way to deal with this in the end. Should the taxpayers have to lower their standard of living for 20 years to pay off mistakes that benefited a small elite?

Stiglitz said governments would survive the shock of such a default because it would uphold the principle of free-market responsibility. 'Counter-parties entered into voluntary agreements with the banks and they must accept the consequences,' he said.

Failed banks have been going bankrupt for hundreds of years; it is the only way to protect the integrity of the system. Why should 4.5 million Irish people have to protect a small elite group of senior bank executives and their boards of directors from the consequences of their own mistakes? The Japanese did this in the 1990s. They kept propping up 'zombie' banks and two decades later they're still trying to recover from the problems caused by not letting any of their banks fail. It kept banks marginally functional through guarantees and piecemeal government bailouts. The resulting 'zombie banks', neither dead nor alive, could not support economic growth. The Irish government's piecemeal approach to the banking crisis has helped financial institutions conceal losses and has favoured shareholders over the taxpayer. Worst of all, it has crippled our credit system just at a time when many Irish businesses are on their knees and are badly in need of credit lines to maintain employment numbers.

In December 2008, the Bank for International Settlements (BIS), which is often called the 'central bank's central bank' because it coordinates transactions between central banks, pointed out that bank rescue packages have transferred significant risks onto government balance sheets, which is reflected in the corresponding widening of sovereign credit default swaps: 'The scope and magnitude of the bank rescue packages also meant that significant risks had been transferred onto government balance sheets.'

In other words, by assuming huge portions of the risk from banks that were trading in toxic securitisation deals and by spending billions that they do not have, Central Banks have put their countries at risk from default.

On 12 March 2008, Bear Sterns bank of New York was allowed to go out of business, by way of a forced sale for a pittance to J. P. Morgan bank, and J. P. Morgan only agreed to the buyout because the government gave them the money to do the deal. Bear Stearns had a banner year in 2006 with $9.2 billion in revenue, and it made $2.05 billion of net income. Yet in 2008 it went out of business.

The huge New York bank Lehman Brothers also went out of business in 2008. When Waterford Wedgwood failed, hundreds of workers, customers, and suppliers were affected, as were their suppliers, workers, etc. Yet this was no reason to bail them out.

They were insolvent so they went out of business: that is the way the system works.

When the free market functions, and failure is allowed, people become instinctively aware of risk, with the result that they voluntarily assume less of it.

Anna Schwartz co-authored with Milton Friedman *A Monetary History of the United States*. It is the definitive account of how misguided monetary policy turned the stock market crash of 1929 into the Great Depression. Federal Reserve Chairman Ben Bernanke has called the 888-page *Monetary History* 'the leading and most persuasive explanation of the worst economic disaster in American history'. Ms Schwartz believes that the US central bankers and Treasury Department are getting it wrong again. To understand why, one first has to understand the nature of the current 'credit market disturbance', as Ms Schwartz delicately calls it. We now hear almost every day that banks will not lend to each other, or will do so only at punitive interest rates. Credit spreads – the difference between what it costs the government to borrow and what private-sector borrowers must pay, are at historic highs, she says, adding that this is not due to a lack of money available to lend, but to a lack of faith in the ability of borrowers to repay their debts. 'The Fed [the US Federal Reserve Bank],' she argues, 'has gone about as if the problem is a shortage of liquidity. That is not the basic problem. The basic problem for the markets is the uncertainty that the balance sheets of financial firms are credible.'

So even though the Fed has flooded the credit markets with cash, spreads haven't budged because banks do not know who is still solvent and who is not. This uncertainty, says Schwartz, is 'the basic problem in the credit market. Lending freezes up when lenders are uncertain that would-be borrowers have the resources to repay them. So to assume that the whole problem is inadequate liquidity bypasses the real issue.'

This is something the Irish government has failed to realise.

In the 1930s, as Schwartz and Friedman argued, the country and the Federal Reserve *was* faced with a liquidity crisis in the banking sector. As banks failed, depositors became alarmed that they would lose their money if their bank, too, failed. So bank runs began, and these became self-reinforcing: 'If the borrowers hadn't withdrawn cash, they [the banks] would have been in good shape. But the Fed just sat by and did nothing, so bank after bank failed. And that only motivated depositors to withdraw funds from banks that were not in distress,' which deepened the crisis and caused still more failures.

But, says Schwartz 'that's not what's going on in the market now'. Today, the banks have a problem on the asset side of their ledgers: 'all these exotic securities that the market does not know how to value.' Why are they 'toxic'? Schwartz says, 'They're toxic because you cannot sell them, you don't know what they're worth, your balance sheet is not credible and the whole market freezes up.'

Former US Secretary of Labor Robert Reich says:

> Despite all the money going directly to the big banks, despite all the government guarantees and loans and special tax breaks, despite the shot-gun weddings and bank mergers, despite the willingness of the Treasury and the Fed to do almost whatever the banks have asked, the reality is that credit is not flowing.
>
> Why? Because the underlying problem with the banks isn't a liquidity problem, the problem is that lenders and investors don't trust they'll get their money back because no one trusts that the numbers

that purport to value securities are anything but wishful thinking.

The trouble, in a nutshell, is that the financial entre-preneurship of recent years – i.e. the derivatives, credit default swaps, collateralised debt instruments, and so on – has undermined all notion of true value.

Many of these fancy instruments became popular over recent years precisely because they circumvented financial regulations, especially rules on banks' capital adequacy. Big banks created all these off-balance-sheet vehicles because they allowed the big banks to carry less capital.

The Irish government should wake up to these facts and stop listening to the bankers, who have run their companies into the ground and will do the same to the Irish economy if the government allows them to. The current Irish banking crisis is not a liquidity problem, it is an *insolvency* problem.

Our government should take the pain; let these failed banks go out of business and start over; it is the only way. Let the fittest survive and the ones which are terminally ill die off.

Otherwise we will be permanently tapped for stimulus packages by failed banks, which will only burden future Irish generations with enormous debts and taxes. The hard reality is that the banks that created this mess have to take their medicine if we are to have any chance of avoiding a deep recession that drags on for years. Some will be wiped out in the process, but propping up banks that have massive quan-tities of toxic debt on their books only delays the inevitable day of reckoning. Bailout plans are a subsidy to investors at taxpayers' expense. Those investors took risks to earn profits and must now also bear the losses. Not every business failure carries systemic risk. The government can ensure a well-functioning financial industry, able to make new loans to creditworthy borrowers, without bailing out particular investors and institutions whose choices proved unwise and flawed. Fundamentally weakening the financial markets in order to calm short-run disruptions is very short-sighted.

The government must cleanse the financial system of those banks which are over-leveraged and holding worthless assets and then create a new, revitalised banking system that works far better than the insolvent one which exists today. The current insolvent banks are the past and a whole new banking institution is the future. To give the existing banks more money is only going to increase the national deficit. There will be no return for the Irish taxpayers, because these banks are going out of business anyway. By continuing to give them more money, we are simply adding to senior bank executives' retirement funds.

In future, we should separate deposit-taking banks from more risky investment banks, whose sophisticated clients should take individual responsibility and run the risk that they might end up losing their shirts. This was the way America's 1933 Glass-Steagall Act worked. That law was passed by the US Congress after the 1929 Depression.

Glass-Steagall survived for more than sixty years prior to being repealed in 1999. The result of that reform was that America's largest retail and commercial banks could use their huge deposit bases from businesses and individuals to engage in mortgage securitisation, and then selling those securities on to investors. It created enormous growth and huge bonuses for a small elite group, but it bankrupted the banking system in the process.

We now need a modern-day Glass-Steagall Act in Ireland to restrain future greedy bankers. Retail banks would then be permitted only to take deposits and lend to individuals and businesses. Investment banks would be allowed to exist, but if they failed, taxpayers would not bail them out.

The major banks have convinced the government that if they go bust the whole financial system will fall. They should be asked to explain that statement. Each bank in turn, AIB, Bank of Ireland and Irish Life, should be asked to explain, in detail, how their demise would be so catastrophic for the Irish economy. We need to know if this is fact, or just fear-mongering.

The banks' problems are not just the reckless loans they made to builders and developers during the property bubble, and their problems are not static; they are growing larger every day. As a result of rising unemployment, estimated at half a million by year end, sub-prime property, prime property, commercial property, credit cards, and car loans are all going to have increasingly high default rates. Even for those still in jobs, the rapid decline in house prices means that people now have no equity left in their houses, and many are even in negative equity. This means that their collateral has been destroyed.

All these problems will block recovery, until some way is found to deal with them. The macro fundamentals are going to trump everything at the end of the day.

We cannot expect our insolvent banks to come up with a solution. They were the ones who created the problem in the first place, by giving ever larger loans to people who had no hope of repaying them, on houses that were grossly overvalued.

Nobody is going to invest in these banks any more because of the massive write-downs they have to face. That is why they have to be allowed to go into bankruptcy.

If a bank is insolvent, creating a 'bad' bank to soak up some of its toxic debt, by transferring these debts to the taxpayers, is only delaying bankruptcy and we will end up with zombie banks on life-support as happened in Japan.

We must decide if we are to continue looking backwards by pouring more taxpayers' money into insolvent banks, with no effect on lending and increasing the national deficit, or if we are finally going to begin looking forward.

To have wasted the time since the banks were saved from bankruptcy in September 2008 means the mountain we have to climb is now so much higher.

Continued failure to confront the bankers and the banking industry, who have brought our economy to its knees, is going to create some very serious questions to be answered by this government.

Most economists predict the world economies will be in recession until the second half of 2010. We should use this period to sort out our credit and banking systems. These are at the very heart of the economy and there should be no more delays in facing up to the fact that our current ethically challenged bankers have no further role to play in the development of the Irish economy.

The current financial crisis has been caused by a lack of transparency by the banks and a lack of regulation by the government; economies which want to be first out of this crisis will need to demonstrate to international investors that they have comprehensively dealt with these two problems.

Ireland needs to purge its financial system of 'crony capitalism' and will have to start with a clean-out of the banking system.

The quality of staff in the new Financial Regulator's office will have to be of much higher calibre than in the past. These will need to be qualified economists, with international banking experience, and not civil-servants, who have dismally failed us in the past.

But by the spring of 2009, there was no transparency on the part of the banks. Their boards of directors were still in place, as were most of their senior executives. They were getting billions in taxpayers' funds, but providing absolutely no information as to how this money was being used. The banks were also borrowing billions from the European Central Bank, and other sources, on the back of the taxpayers' guarantee and we also had zero information as to how these incredible amounts of money were being used. The banks were also failing to disclose the level and nature of their toxic debts.

This was an appalling situation and the government was completely to blame, as they were the only ones with the power to rectify the problem.

The banks had no notion of reforming, or introducing transparency in their dealings. They were simply continuing to bleed the Irish economy dry without any accountability whatsoever and the government stood idly by. They seemed afraid to ask the bankers anything, and when they needed answers to questions they hired expensive accountancy firms to ask the questions for them. The government was making no attempt to determine which banks were solvent and which were not.

This could have been very easily done by compelling the banks to disclose the true value of their toxic debts. They should have required the banks to auction a sample of these debts as a means of determining their true value. If a bank is insolvent and even if they sell their debts at true long-term value, they are still going to be under water.

The Irish economy will not recover until we have a properly transparent banking system and the sooner we get to grips with this problem, the sooner we will have recovery.

A lot of solutions need to be applied to a lot of problems in the Irish economy, but nothing will begin to work until the banking system is reformed.

Irish bankers gambled massively and lost, they must now pay the penalty for having lost.

Any Irish government which attempts to transfer these massive gambling debts on to the Irish taxpayers should be driven from office and not allowed into government again in the lifetime of this generation.

Chapter 11

OUR LEADERS – WITHOUT GOOD LEADERSHIP WE ARE LOST

Men make history, and not the other way around.
In periods where there is no leadership, society stands still.
Progress occurs when courageous, skillful leaders seize the
opportunity to change things for the better.

US President Harry Truman

Ireland can get out of the current mess it finds itself in, but we have to make the right decisions and there is no room for any more mistakes. A large part of this book is devoted to some of the mistakes we made over the past ten years as it is necessary to face these facts before we can go forward.

With our economy reeling, some politicians and business leaders are saying 'let's not play the blame game' and 'it's time to move on'. Well, that just won't wash. Otherwise we will run the risk of repeating those same mistakes all over again.

We need to take a long, hard look in the mirror and stop kidding ourselves that we are blessed with the 'luck o' the Irish' and that we'll get through the current crisis no matter what. We won't: it will only happen if we decide to make it happen.

It is perfectly true to say that Ireland would survive even if we did very little to sort out the current crisis. But in what way would it survive? More than likely it would be as a poor nation that once had a great future but as a result of corrupt roguery and very bad government economic decisions, it squandered a bright future for its people and burdened its children with billions in debt.

It is still a possibility that Ireland will end up that way. This is why we must now examine every decision that our peers make, in a much more enquiring way than we have previously done.

We cannot trust our politicians to tell us the truth, because they have lied to us in the past.

We cannot trust our bankers because they have also lied to us repeatedly, in addition to running their banks into the ground and causing the destruction of the wealth of a generation in the process.

We must now trust ourselves and have confidence in our own abilities and judgments.

The first and biggest test on that road is one of leadership.

Without good leadership we are lost

Ireland currently does not have good leadership. This was verified on 31 March 2009, when Ireland was finally stripped of its very valuable AAA credit rating by international credit rating agency Standard & Poor's. Global head of sovereign ratings, David Beers, was worried that a credible 'fiscal strategy' would not emerge until after the next general election.

Our current political leaders are the ones who got us into this mess and they should now leave the stage. If they had any decency they would be gone long ago. They are yesterday's men and women and are not capable of leading us to the Promised Land.

Our current political leaders have a smug 'I'm-all-right-Jack' air about them and, considering how they have feathered their own nests over the past ten years, it is easy to understand why they have such a self-satisfied air about them. These same leaders all looked fine up until September 2008, when the government was presented with the appalling decision of having to make the Irish taxpayers accept liability for the combined debts (€485 billion) of all the major Irish banks. That was the moment when Irish people finally realised that their leaders didn't have a clue what was going on.

All through the summer of 2008 our political and banking leaders had been telling us everything was fine and we had nothing to worry about. They trotted out their 'the fundamentals are sound' mantra ad nauseam on a daily basis. But they were the only ones who held that view as was evidenced by the daily collapse in the share prices of all our major banks.

We all discovered in September 2008 that the fundamentals were far from sound and the thing that disturbed most intelligent people was that our leaders were so totally oblivious to the dangers at hand.

We must never again allow a situation like that to develop.

We must never again assume that the people we elect have the necessary intelligence to run the country properly simply because we voted for them along party lines. We must be much more discerning in how we cast our votes in future.

We must now pay very close attention to who is going to replace these current leaders who have let the country down so badly. The way our political system works is that we vote for the TDs and they vote for the leaders. We must very objectively examine the qualities of the leader they select and if we are not happy with those qualities we must penalise that party at the ballot box, right across the country, if we decide that they have made a bad decision. This is the only way to ensure that we are going to get competent political leadership.

At this point in our history we most certainly do not want a political leader whose main qualification for the job is that '*it's their turn*' – that approach would spell disaster.

What qualities do we require in good political leaders at this point in our history?

Leadership is only really tested when times are tough. In the good times, when things were plentiful, a man like Brian Cowen looked competent enough. But when the pressure came on, his deficiencies were very quickly exposed. No original ideas, bad communication skills, a reliance on cronies for advice and staggering from one daily crisis to the next providing ill-thought-out, knee-jerk responses and acting the bully as a substitute for reasoned debate. It reminds me of the saying 'anybody can play a good hand well, but it's being able to play a bad hand well that counts.'

An army of sheep led by a lion would defeat an army of lions led by a sheep.

Arab proverb

Ireland is now in a period of 'adaptive change', i.e. the sort of change that occurs when people are forced to adjust to a radically altered environment. In such an environment they must challenge the traditional understanding of the leader–follower relationship.

Conventional thinking holds that leaders protect their followers from harsh surroundings and events. But in times of adaptive change leaders who truly care for their followers expose them to the painful reality of existing conditions and demand that they themselves fashion an appropriate response. Instead of giving people false assurances that their best is good enough, leaders in such times must insist that people surpass themselves. And rather than smoothing over conflicts, leaders force disputes to the surface. This is something that is urgently needed in a few very important areas of Irish society at present. Adaptive change carries emotional costs, but the cultivation of emotional fortitude creates well-being instead of comfort and thereby allows people to realise their maximum potential very quickly. Adaptive change is required when our deeply held beliefs are challenged, when the values that made us successful become less relevant. Adaptive problems are often systemic problems with no ready answers. Mobilising people to adapt their behaviour in order to thrive in the new environment is critical. Without such change, failure to achieve maximum potential is guaranteed.

So the mark of leadership in the new, competitive world that Ireland now finds itself in is in getting the Irish people to engage in adaptive change. What worked yesterday will not work today and most certainly will not work tomorrow. We must begin anew.

In order to make this change happen, we have to break a long-standing behaviour pattern of expecting leadership to provide solutions. The focus of responsibility for problem solving must shift to all of us. Solutions to adaptive challenges reside in the collective intelligence of all players in the game, and in teamwork, where we all use one another as resources and learn our way to solutions. (The success such collaborative effort can bring was gloriously displayed by our victorious rugby team in the spring of 2009.)

Adaptive change is not easy for the people going through it. They need to take on new roles, new relationships, new values, new behaviours, and new approaches to work and life in general. In such situations, rather than fulfilling the expectation that they will provide answers, leaders have to ask tough questions. Rather than protecting people from outside threats, leaders should allow them to feel the bite of reality in order to stimulate them to adapt.

In times of adaptive change, instead of maintaining norms, a good leader makes us challenge the old ways which no longer work and get us to face up to practices that must be discarded.

There is nothing wrong with having social workers, small town solicitors and court barristers running the country, that's how democracy works. But right now, at this crucial point in Ireland's history, we need leaders of a higher calibre. We need leaders with hard-earned, real-life experience in economic policy and direct hands-on experience in the cauldron of commerce. Both these levels of experience should be of a very high quality. The challenge is too great to settle for anything less. Because anything less will lead us to failure.

At a time like this Ireland needs leaders who can give the people a strong sense of the history of the situation and what is good about its past, as well as an idea of the market forces at work today and the personal responsibility people must take in shaping the nation's future. They must watch for the many functional and dysfunctional reactions to change. They must be able to motivate people to high performance at a time when money is scarce.

There are always four hurdles which block achievement in such situations: people in current positions of power who want the status quo, limited resources, an unmotivated workforce and opposition from powerful vested interests.

There is a leadership insight that, in any organisation, once the beliefs and energies of a critical mass of people are engaged, conversion to a new idea will spread like an epidemic, bringing about fundamental change very quickly. The theory suggests that such a movement can be unleashed only by a leader who can make unforgettable and unarguable calls for change (a great communicator), who concentrates his or her resources on what really matters, who mobilises the commitment of the people, and who succeeds in silencing the most vocal critics.

Our new leaders need to be able to do these things. Most leaders only dream of pulling off this kind of performance, but the right person can make the dream become reality.

> *I am looking for a lot of men who have an infinite capacity to not know what can't be done.*
>
> **Henry Ford**

Former Taoiseach Bertie Ahern

Less than year after winning a third term, Bertie Ahern stood down as Taoiseach. At his various tribunal appearances Ahern maintained he had done nothing wrong. But Fianna Fáil party sources realised that questions about undeclared corporate donations had made him a liability.

2006: Ahern said that he had listened for seven years to warnings and arguments about difficulties in the construction sector: 'I think you have to look at the asset. This is the question: if you are borrowing 'x', if you sell the asset, if there's a bit of a downturn, will you get 'x' back in return? That's the issue. At the moment, there doesn't seem to be an indication [of difficulties]. I mean quite frankly, if you had taken the advice a year ago you would have lost a lot of money. Everybody said we're going to see a huge downturn in 2005 linking into 2006 – they were entirely wrong. Really, we should have an examination into why so many people got it so wrong. My view is there's not a great problem. Really, the bad advice of last year given by so many has maybe made some people make mistakes when they should have bought last year.'

2007: 'On the other side of the election we'll get back to normality. And I think that normality will be the soft landing. The construction projections were that we will move from something like 93,000 houses to 80-something. Now that's not going to create any kind of a difficulty.'

2007: 'Sitting on the sidelines, cribbing and moaning is a lost opportunity. I don't know how people who engage in that don't commit suicide because frankly the only thing that motivates me is being able to actively change something.'

2007: 'But there is no place for negativity. No need for any pessimism. Above all, there is no place for politically motivated attempts to talk down the economy.'

Taoiseach Brian Cowen

2007 (when he was Finance Minister): 'There is an adjustment taking place against the background of the very high house-price inflation we saw over the last decade, which was not sustainable.' He added that there were 'no indications' of an increase in bad debts and defaults by homeowners.

2008 – on a visit to the US: 'We are now a prosperous and peaceful country. That enables us to face the future with confidence.'

2008 – on the huge government borrowing requirement in 2009 for day-to-day spending: 'This is not sustainable or sensible. It risks a return to a debt spiral where interest payments consume ever increasing amounts of taxation. None of us want to repeat the mistakes of the 1980s.'

2008 – on his pay increase of €38,000: 'It would be hypocritical not to accept it.'

2008 – On large bonuses for business leaders: 'I have problems with that . . .'

2008 – 'We face stark choices. If we do not make the right ones, it will have catastrophic consequences.'

Chapter 12

POLITICIANS' SALARIES –
ASTONISHING

There is a very good reason why only a small number of Irish TDs have anything to say on the current economic crisis. Over the past ten years, few sectors of Irish society have done better in pay terms than the politicians – of all parties. In the public sector the politicians have been the biggest gainers both in pay and expense increases.

The average earnings of an Irish TD is around €110,000 (roughly the same pay as a United States senator). Some members of the Dáil draw almost as much again in tax-free unvouched expenses.

Ireland has 166 TDs, who represent 4.2 million people. This is one TD for every 25,000 people – four times as many as in the UK in proportional terms. New Zealand, with a similar population as Ireland (4.1m), has 120 Members of Parliament.

POLITICIANS' SALARIES – ASTONISHING

The budget for the Houses of the Oireachtas (Parliament and Senate) for 2009 is to rise 12.3 per cent, an increase of 61 per cent in five years.

Some 20 per cent of the members employ their own family as personal assistants.

TDs and senators receive daily pocket money to attend the sittings of the Dáil and Senate, in addition to their unvouched and untaxed expenses.

In the seven years between 1999 and 2006, pay for TDs increased by 119 per cent. That averages at increases of 17 per cent per year over the period. Our politicians also enjoy superior 'gold-plated' pension benefits – for a pension contribution of 6 per cent of salary – based on half their final salary and with a 'golden handshake' payment of one and a half times their salary. So if a TD with twenty years' service retired today, he/she would get a pension of €1,110 per week and a golden handshake of €160,000.

Pay rates for politicians

President	€333,000	–	€6,900 per week.
Taoiseach	€287,617	–	€5,990 per week.
Ministers	€240,000	–	€5,000 per week.
Junior ministers	€165,000	–	€3,450 per week.

There is also a tax break exclusively for members of the government, which allows ministers to claim relief on second homes and for overnight accommodation in Dublin.

Government ministers also get an additional office staff allowance.

Tánaiste Mary Coughlan and Health Minister Mary Harney have by far the biggest wage bill for personal assistants, spending almost €2.5 million between them on secretaries and advisers. Ministers Coughlan and Harney, who have argued strongly for cutbacks, are by far the most generous ministers when it comes to wages for their own staff.

Minister for the Environment and Green Party leader, John Gormley, employs fifteen people in all, including part-time staff, nine in his private office, at a salary cost of upwards of €590,335. Non-salary staff expenses in Gormley's department last year amounted to €128,635.

Minister Coughlan: will spend over €1.3 million in 2009 on eighteen assistants, secretaries and advisers. Fifteen people work in the Tánaiste's private government office and three in her constituency office in Donegal. These each get paid an average of €74,123 per year – €1,500 per week.

Minister Harney: In addition to her salary of €5,000 per week will spend more than €1 million on fourteen staff, eleven employed in her private office and three in her constituency office. These are paid an average of €81,357 per year each – €1,700 per week.

Minister Harney's department employs the most assistants, even though the vast majority of its work has been passed to the Health Service Executive.

Taoiseach Brian Cowen: In addition to his personal salary of €5,990 per week, he will also spend over €1 million for twenty-two staff, fourteen in his private office and eight in his constituency office, in Tullamore.

Junior Minister for Europe Dick Roche has thirteen assistants employed at a cost of €638,576 a year.

Minister Martin Cullen has ten private office and constituency staff, costing €655,000.

Oddly, Minister Eamonn O'Cuiv has twelve staff who, at €218,923, cost only a third of Cullen's ten staff.

When cost savings in the Health Service Executive (HSE) are discussed by the government, cutbacks in services to the long suffering taxpayers are the only solution put forward – cutbacks in the huge wage bill are never mentioned.

With pay rises and tax-free expense accounts, TDs cost the Irish taxpayers around €40 million in 2008. In 2009, 166 TDs will receive around €110,000 in their basic salary, in addition to a €43,000 expense account and a €23,000 travel expenses account, so they will get a total of around €3,650 per week each.

TDs and senators salaries

TDs and senators of all parties (Fianna Fáil, Fine Gael, Labour, PDs, Sinn Fein and Independents) get paid the same and draw the same 'gold-plated' pensions.

In 1997, a TD was paid €44,067; by 2008 this had increased to over €100,000. New Zealand pays its Members of Parliament the equivalent of €56,730.

TDs are paid €110,000 – €2,220 per week. They are paid 40% more than British MPs who make €71,000 (approx.) per annum. Most backbench TDs receive allowances on top of their salary for serving as chairs, vice-chairs or whips on one of the more than twenty Oireachtas committees. Such a benefit can add another €45,000 per annum to a TD's salary.

Senators are paid €74,607　　　—　　　€1,555 per week.

The Cathaoirleach of the Seanad gets €119,388
　　　　　　　　　　—　　　€2,485 per week.

Senators also receive expenses of €24,700, a secretarial allowance of €40,100 and travel expenses of €32,300. So the actual total income for a senator is €171,700
　　　　　　　　　　—　　　€4,088 per week.

Fine Gael leader Enda Kenny announced a self-imposed 5 per cent pay cut in 2008. But unlike most other TDs, Kenny has two alternative sources of income, both funded by the taxpayer: he collects a ministerial pension and his Mercedes car, plus driver and expenses which are covered from the party's state allowance. Last year, his pension was worth just short of €15,000 and the leader's expenses package cost €48,000 from the Fine Gael leader's allowance. So he gets an additional €63,000 a year, which brings his total income to €169,567, or €3,500 per week. It is very easy to take a 5 per cent pay cut (€175 per week) when you are making that kind of money.

But at least he made some effort.

Chapter 13

PUBLIC SECTOR SALARIES – INCREDIBLE

Over the past ten years Ireland has lived through the greatest period of prosperity in the history of the state. But a third of a million of our citizens are now out of work and surviving on dole of €204 per week.

How can this be reconciled with public sector workers who have been awarded salary increases for 2009 which will cost the Irish taxpayers €600 million?

Over the coming years, as this recession bites ever deeper, many thousands more will end up on the dole and they will be virtually all from the private sector, as public sector jobs are guaranteed.

In the public sector it is practically impossible to lose your job and even if you did, you would probably receive a handsome severance package and full 'gold-plated' pension entitlements.

What exactly are our public sector workers paid?

The public sector pay and pensions bill was set out in the Pre-Budget Estimates for 2008 at over €18.6 billion (that's eighteen thousand six hundred million euro, a truly staggering figure). This would rise to €20 billion in 2009. (While there was an adjustment to this figure as a result of the pension levy early in 2009, that would seem to be have been offset somewhat by the announcement at the start of May 2009 that the government had set aside a quarter of a billion euro to fund public sector pay increments – not exactly a wholehearted attempt on the part of the government to rein in the public sector pay and pensions cost!)

The European Commission's EUROSTAT data show that, in Ireland, the average public sector employee earned over 20 per cent more than workers in the private sector.

The data also show that Irish public servants are more highly paid than their counterparts in each of the countries reviewed: Germany, Denmark, Netherlands, Finland and the UK.

An average teacher's salary in Ireland in 2004 was found to be 25 per cent higher than in Germany and 35 per cent higher than in the UK.

Health and social workers in Ireland earned an average of 30 per cent ahead of those in the UK and nearly double the average earnings for the sector in Finland.

They also found that the Irish income tax burden of public sector workers is the lowest in the OECD and, when public sector wages are examined on an after-tax basis, the pay premium enjoyed by the Irish public sector rises to over 50 per cent.

PUBLIC SECTOR SALARIES – INCREDIBLE

Research from the European Central Bank (ECB) found that between 1999 and 2006, average public sector pay in Ireland increased by 67 per cent, which in the rest of the Eurozone grew by just 22 per cent.

Irish public sector pay has grown faster than any other country in the EU and actual pay levels have overtaken those in almost every other OECD country.

Average hourly pay of Irish public sector workers is almost 50 per cent higher than those in the private sector.

The National Employment Survey, which was carried out in October 2006 by the Central Statistics Office (CSO), reveals the average hourly earnings of workers in the public sector are 48.9 per cent higher than workers in the private sector. Public sector earnings average €25.47 per hour, compared with €17.11 per hour in the private sector, according to the CSO.

The highest earners in terms of hourly pay are workers in the education sector, who average €32.06 per hour. The average working week is 34.8 hours, with men working 38.3 hours and women 31 hours. Teachers have the shortest working week, with just 26.7 hours per week.

A loss of competitiveness in the private sector gets remedied by either wage adjustment or job reductions. Such mechanisms are not applied within the public sector.

Building permanent costs like these into public sector pay and pensions was nothing short of scandalous and will cripple Ireland's future prospects unless they are reversed.

The demands of the public sector unions and the acquiescence of our self-serving politicians to these demands have directly opened up the 'emigrant trail' as the only option, once more, for the young people of Ireland. Our politicians, who engineered this, should hang their heads in shame at what is a disgraceful episode in our young nation's history.

Chapter 14

PUBLIC SECTOR PENSIONS – GOLD-PLATED

In January 2009, Finance Minister Brian Lenihan revealed in the Dáil that pre-1995 civil servants pay nothing for their personal pension entitlements. They are also entitled to receive their public service pensions *in addition to their state pensions*.

A secretary-general in the civil service retiring after forty years on basic earnings of €221,929 (€4,623 per week) is entitled to a lump-sum golden handshake of €332,894.

In addition, he or she will then receive an index-linked pension of €110,964 (€2,311 per week) for life and any time the current holder of the job from which he or she retired from gets a pay rise, his or her pension will increase by the same amount.

According to the Report of the Commission on Public Service Pensions, the future cost of the public sector pensions will be €1,737,000,000 (€1.737 billion) in 2012 and will rise to €3,058,000,000 (€3.058 billion) by 2027. These are truly incredible figures and an absolute disgrace with over 1 million Irish people having no pension of any sort bar the old-age pension. Such pensions are unheard of in the private sector.

Irish public sector pensions the most generous in the world

In December 2008, in a study by academic actuaries of University College Dublin, Drs Whelan and Moloney, for the Society of Actuaries of Ireland, from calculations based on the 2007 Benchmarking Report, found that public sector pensions in Ireland are the most generous in the world.

This is a result of these pensions being state guaranteed and often payable from the age of sixty.

Public sector pensions are also linked to the salary at the time of retirement. This means the pension rises with pay agreements and other pay rises, unlike private sector pensions. Whelan and Moloney's report found that Ireland's exposure to the pension promises already made to public servants is over €100 billion and not €70 million as has been claimed by the 'Report of the Public Service Benchmarking Body 2007'. It is a scandal that this situation should have been allowed to develop. The civil servants have certainly ensured that they will have a luxury retirement at the expense of the Irish taxpayer.

Most public sector workers only pay around 5 to 6 per cent of their salary to fund their pensions.

The Whelan/Moloney report points out that the cost to the state of providing a public sector pension is actually 30 per cent of a public servant's salary. So the Irish taxpayers end up paying the additional 25 per cent to cover these 'gold-plated' pensions.

The reasons for the high value attached to public sector pensions is that there is no risk that a worker in the public sector will not be paid, unlike in the private sector where there are huge investment losses: many invested in Irish bank shares and have practically been wiped out.

In December 2008, Minister Mary Hanafin announced: *'Over 1 million, or nearly half of all workers, do not have a private or occupational pension and may be entirely reliant on the State pension when they retire.'* This is in stark contrast to the 'gold-plated pensions' our politicians have organised for themselves, paid for by the taxpayers. Including Minister Hanafin's own pension.

Minister Hanafin informed the Cabinet that several schemes could collapse as the pension deficit reaches €30 billion. She also said some under-funded schemes could collapse in the next six months, with an estimated 50 per cent failing within a year. She also warned that some schemes would not be able to pay out on the benefits they had originally promised. She pointed out that some defined benefit pension schemes, in the private sector, were facing collapse and that up to 90 per cent of defined benefit schemes are in deficit. The worst affected will be those approaching retirement age, who may only get a fraction of what they had planned for. She went on to say that budgetary constraints would make it impossible for the government to make up the shortfall if schemes collapsed.

So the politicians are washing their hands of the matter. They say they have no money. But in December 2008, the government was able to give €180 million in compensation to the pig processors for the loss of one week's production, in spite of the fact that the entire pork industry is worth only €368 million in an entire year. (If Department of Agriculture inspectors were doing their job properly this situation would not have arisen in the first place. But the Department of Agriculture inspectors are part of the public service so it had no effect whatsoever on their salaries and 'gold-plated' pensions, which are cast in stone. Just give the bill to the Irish taxpayer).

The whole situation is practically unbelievable.

Bertie Ahern is currently drawing a pension of over €150,000 p.a. – €3,125 per week – from his time as Taoiseach. In addition to this he is also currently drawing his TD's salary of over €2,200 per week.

This gives him a combined weekly income of €5,325 per week.

His time in the 'public service' has made him a rich man, far richer than 95 per cent of Irish people.

His work on behalf of the 'social partners' (the public sector unions), has benefited himself handsomely. All those late nights hammering out deals have certainly seen him feather his own nest and become a very wealthy man. Based on current annuity rates, a private sector worker would need to purchase an annuity, or have a personal pension fund, amounting to €4.5 million to guarantee a pension of €146,000 per year payable from the age of fifty. Is this fair and just, where a third of a million of Irish people are living on €204 a week dole and the only the basic state old-age pension to look forward to when they retire?

Despite earnings of up to €200,000 a year, serving politicians are entitled to ministerial pensions. Five current cabinet ministers, who have more than ten years' service, will qualify for the full ministerial pension when they retire from government and will more than likely be drawing a TD's salary of over €100,000 also. These are Brian Cowen, Micheál Martin, Noel Dempsey, Mary Harney and Dermot Ahern.

The 2008 pay increases government ministers voted for themselves will add up to €500,000 to the value of a minister's pension.

Yes. They certainly know how to look after themselves.

Three senior government ministers have kept their teaching positions in their former schools open, with full pension rights, despite being full-time politicians for between eleven and twenty-one years. They are Minister Noel Dempsey, Minister Micheál Martin, and Minister Mary Hanafin.

Two current serving TDs are in receipt of teaching pensions, although they have not taught for thirty-three years. They are Fine Gael leader Enda Kenny and Fianna Fáil's Michael Kitt. Like other long-serving Oireachtas members, they have accrued full pension rights in addition to being entitled to generous Dáil and ministerial pensions.

All benefit from a long-standing arrangement for teachers who are TDs and senators. The scheme permits a replacement teacher to be employed, with the cost of the replacement's salary being deducted from the teacher's salary of the TD or senator. The TD is entitled to the difference between both salaries.

There are additional hard-to-believe benefits for the politician in that the teaching job is kept open and full pension entitlements *continue to accrue*, irrespective of how long the TD or senator has been absent from their school or college. Thirty sitting TDs are currently on leave from teaching positions. Only one TD has resigned a teaching position with no pension rights. That was Trevor Sargent (Green Party) who stood down from his national school position during his second Dáil term.

In 2006 the government's finance accounts showed that thirty-four then sitting TDs and senators were in receipt of ministerial pensions, earning an average of €15,143 on top of their Oireachtas income.

Under a politician's pension terms, a person with at least two years' service in a ministerial office qualifies for a pension. Although pensions are not normally payable until the person concerned reaches the age of fifty-five, a former minister aged between fifty and fifty-five can claim a discounted pension.

Since 1993, there are some restrictions on serving politicians drawing their ministerial pension. Pensions are now 'abated,' to use a civil service term, by a half 'for as long as the recipient remains in the Dáil, Seanad or European Parliament'. But the rise in ministerial salaries and an increase in the percentage of income that a former minister is entitled to in pension payments more than compensates for this. The amount of pension to which a politician is entitled is directly linked to the length of time they spend in ministerial office: two years in office entitles the minister to 20 per cent of salary, increasing to 60 per cent for ten or more years. There is nothing even remotely similar to that in the private sector.

As of December 2008, seven members of the current cabinet had passed the ten-year mark in senior ministerial office and qualify for 60 per cent pensions once they cease being ministers (although, of course, half will be 'abated' for as long as they are in the Dáil). This is what the 'brilliant' all-night deals with the *social partners*' produced.

TDs pay 6 per cent of their salary to fund their pensions; this entitles them to a full pension after just twenty years. In the UK, MPs pay a pension contribution of 10 per cent of salary towards their pensions. No wonder our politicians are 'removed' from the majority of Irish workers and from reality.

In 2006, the Pensions Ombudsman Paul Kenny warned that around 130,000 construction workers were not covered for pensions or sick pay benefits. Kenny criticised construction companies for failing to make contributions to pension funds on behalf of workers. How will these people now manage, given that many of them are on the dole and the companies they worked for have been wound up?

At the end of 2008, Kenny said he was dealing with half a dozen cases of building workers who died on the job, but their families were unable to draw death-in-service benefits because the employer had not paid in the contributions.

Our politicians are paid huge salaries to see that this does not happen. They have failed in their 'duty of care' to Irish private sector workers in having allowed the current situation to develop. No doubt they will trot out their usual mantra 'this is caused by external forces beyond our control'. But the politicians made sure their own pensions were in no danger. Those will be paid in full by the Irish taxpayers, most of whom will end up with no pension themselves.

What happened to the money that was paid into private sector pension funds?

The politicians say that the catastrophe in the private sector pensions is 'the result of recent market turmoil'. That is not true. Because the average annual return by Irish pension funds over the past ten years was only 1.9 per cent per annum. If they had lodged those funds in the Post Office they would have got a better return. Yet the government seems to have spotted this problem only at the end of 2008. There now needs to be, as a matter of urgency, a thorough investigation into how the pension funds invested Irish people's money over the past five years. We need an explanation as to why the return on these funds was so low, and an exposure of the pay and bonuses of the senior executives at these pension companies over the past five years, as they managed these accounts. The first funds to be investigated should be the ones which have connections to the Irish banks. This sort of investigation is vital if we are to restore confidence in our financial services sector.

On 30 November 2008 Brian Cowen, in relation to private sector pension schemes, said: 'They were affected by market fluctuations. Obviously, the Minister for Social and Family Affairs will be engaging with the pensions industry to review their funding arrangements and work with them in the coming months on long-term strategies.'

PUBLIC SECTOR PENSIONS – GOLD-PLATED

It is high time our government did a lot more than 'engage' with these pension funds.

Cowen went on to say: 'These are turbulent times for money markets, where most private sector pension funds are invested. Pension fund managers have yet to report on their funding standards to the Irish Pensions Board, but they have indicated that funds are subject to market fluctuations.'

Pension fund managers, in addition to the bankers, must not be allowed to regulate themselves. They must be compelled to open their books to independent investigation and any wrongdoing which is uncovered needs to be prosecuted to the full extent of the law.

Taking guff from these pension fund executives – such as 'funds are subject to market fluctuations' – should no longer be tolerated. I wonder were their salaries and bonuses subject to the same 'fluctutations'.

Irish politicians were well able to protect their own pensions from 'external forces' and 'turbulent times'. But in the meantime they have committed hundreds of thousands of Irish workers to a long, grim period of struggle in their old age. They will be forced to exist on the state's old-age pension, despite a lifetime of contributions to private pension schemes. That our government should have allowed this to happen is disgraceful.

Irish Public Sector Pensions (which include the politicians) have been described as being amongst the best in the world. For a private sector worker to have the equivalent benefit of a public sector pension, it would require funding of an estimated 25 per cent of annual salary every year for forty years.

Incredible benefits

There are 370,000 people employed in the public sector who are living lives of a privileged and wealthy elite.

Ireland's Chief Justice is paid €7,600 per week. He receives an annual salary of €295,915 – €6,165 per week. On retirement he will be entitled to a 'gold-plated' public sector pension which will be worth up to 60 per cent of his salary – €3,700 per week – and a 'golden handshake' of one and a half times his final salary, which will come to €444,000. He is also being paid a pension for his two terms as Attorney General. Because that pension is linked to the current Attorney General's pay level – €219,000 – he received €69,042 in 2007 from the state as a pension. This gives him a public sector income for 2007 of €365,000 – €7,600 per week. But he also draws another pension entitlement from his time on the European Court of Justice. It would cost almost €10 million to fund his pension if he was in the private sector.

In November 2008 Taoiseach Brian Cowen said in an interview with *Hot Press* magazine: 'If we try to ride out this recession as if it is not affecting us or shouldn't affect us, then we won't be competitive, we won't be able to increase our exports, we won't be able to generate the wealth to get us back on track.' He said the public has not yet grasped the gravity of the situation facing the country, in what he described as 'the most severe global economic and financial conditions for a century'. This illustrates how out of touch with reality our Taoiseach is. Those in the private sector know only too well what the situation is, because they are the ones who are suffering and not Brian Cowen, who is earning €6,000 per week and has a 'government-guaranteed gold-plated pension' to look forward to when he retires. This recession will have very few consequences for the public sector, of which he is a member.

Chapter 15

SHOCKING WASTE – A WHIFF OF CORRUPTION

The Amber Room, Katherine Palace, St Petersburg, Russia

The Amber Room was commissioned by Frederick I of Prussia in 1701, and later was presented to Czar Peter the Great. Considered one of the greatest of Europe's missing treasures, the Amber Room – often described as the 'Eighth Wonder of the World' – is currently valued at about $250 million. It consisted of 100,000 pieces of carved amber panelling covering the walls of the room.

In 1941, when Nazi troops were approaching Leningrad, hasty preparations were made to evacuate the most precious exhibits to a safer place. But the Amber Room was too fragile, so a decision was made to hide it under double walls with paintings of low value over them. When the German troops occupied the Katherine Palace, the trick was disclosed. They dismantled the Amber Room and shipped it to Eastern Prussia – Kenigsberg, now the Russian port city of Kalinigrad. All traces of the Amber Room then vanished.

After nearly fifty years the Russian government gave up all hope of relocating the panels and initiated the reconstruction of the Amber Room. Two fragments of the chamber were discovered in Germany in 2000: a Florentine mosaic and a chest of drawers. Germany returned them to Russia. Highly skilled craftspeople worked tirelessly on the project, using microscopes to make the tiniest engravings in the amber. Amber is the fossilised resin of now-extinct trees and 1 kg of top-quality amber costs about $250 on world markets. The restoration work consumed six tons of amber. Every metre of this immense work of art is made up of between 800 to 1,000 pieces of amber. The replica of the Amber Room was unveiled in 2003 in time for St Petersburg's 300th-anniversary celebrations.

Total cost: $11 million (approximately €7.9 million).

Refurbishment of Cork Courthouse

Total cost: €26 million

The refurbishment began in April 2003. The project took twenty months to complete and was re-opened in 2005. The original estimate for the work in 1995 was €6.35 million.

Eventual cost, €26 million. The cost overrun was explained as follows: 'Construction inflation between 1995 and 2003 amounted to a 60 per cent increase which increased the figure to €10.16 million. The balance (€15.84 million) was made up by the cost of the design team, site investigations, furniture, fittings and equipment, contingency, etc.'

The Central Statistics Office (CSO) says that the Irish inflation rate over this period was 30 per cent.

Dublin Port Tunnel

Total cost: €752 million

Twin tunnels, 2.8 miles in length and a total project length of 3.5 miles. That equates to €214.8 million per mile.

The tender price for construction of the tunnel was €457 million, but the final project cost was a mind-blowing €752 million. This cost overrun (€295 million) was explained as follows: 'Land acquisition, design, insurance, legal and other services, plus supervision.'

In spring 2006, media reports revealed that the tunnel was leaking substantial amounts of water, which was discovered to be as a result of substandard concrete being poured.

There's more: In 1987, the Minister for Transport sold a small – but pivotal – piece of land to the private company National Toll Roads (NTR) for €14 million (in 2008 terms). In February 2007, the Minister bought it back for €600 million which will be paid in annual instalments of €50 million. The final figure for this transaction will be nearer to a billion, when the cost-of-living clause is invoked by NTR.

E-voting machines (which were never used)

Total cost (to date): €62 million

Storing e-voting machines cost €850,000 in 2007, despite the fact that they have not been used, and will not be used. The initial cost of the machines was €53.1 million, including the €2.6 million spent on public-awareness campaigns. The plan to use them for voting was shelved when security concerns were raised, and they have been stored ever since. Returning officers in individual constituencies took the responsibility for renting space to store them, but that cost, funded by the taxpayer, has run into millions of euro to date. The breakdown of individual yearly storage is:

€658,000 in 2004
€696,000 in 2005
€706,000 in 2006
€528,000 in 2007

There have to be changes in how accountability is established in these types of situations.

New Terminal at Dublin Airport

Total cost: €395 million

In 2005, the government gave the go-ahead for the building of the new terminal at Dublin Airport, capable of handling 15 million passengers per year. It was to cost €270 million, including the additional cost of site preparation and support infrastructure such as roadways, aprons and contact stands.

In May 2005, the Dublin Airport Authority (DAA) said: 'The timeline for the development of a second terminal is likely to extend over three and a half to four years. The DAA will first consult with its airline customers to ascertain what type of facility they require to cater for their forecast volumes and mix of traffic. This will help determine the most appropriate site, scope and design of the terminal building and support infrastructure. As soon as the specification is finalised, DAA is committed to having the scope and costing of the project submitted for independent verification, before proceeding to the planning process and subsequent tender process.'

In August 2006, the DAA announced that the terminal would cost €395 million, i.e. 46 per cent higher (€125 million) than forecast one year earlier.

In 2005, an airline terminal of similar size was opened at the ultra-modern Kuala Lumpur airport, in Malaysia.

It took less than a year to build and cost only €27 million. But a similar terminal in Ireland was budgeted to cost €395 million.

Chapter 16

DEFLATION – THE KILLER BLOW

There is no deflation threat in Europe.
Jean-Claude Trichet February 2009

O h, really?

In February 2009, the Central Statistics Office said that Ireland had an annual inflation rate of –0.1 per cent for January. This was the first time the country had negative inflation since 1960. Our rate of inflation for March was even worse at –2.6 per cent. This was the lowest level since 1933. Ireland is now facing into deflation for the first time in more than seventy years.

But the government is unwilling to acknowledge that the debt crisis is a reflection of long-term problems and not just an isolated phenomenon. With the announcement of the latest figures they told us that, when house prices were exempted, the figures were fine. Of course, this was the very same government that told us five years previously, during the property bubble, that if you exempted house prices the inflation figures were fine and the economy was in great shape.

And what was the Irish government's priority in April 2009, as the spectre of deflation loomed large? Bailing out the property speculators and bankers who wrecked the economy in the first place, to the tune of €90 billion, instead of using those funds to reduce the burden of residential mortgage debt for every householder in the country.

But as Brian Cowen had already bellowed in the Dáil, 'I'll run the country the way I see fit,' even though he knows (or should know by now) that his actions are going to seal the deal on a deflationary future for Ireland.

The warning signs were evident everywhere, neither Cowen nor his Finance Minister Lenihan would be able to say this time that 'nobody saw it coming'. Brian Cowen will go down in history as the worst Taoiseach this country ever had, especially if he turns recession into depression which is looking more likely with every day he remains in office.

The €90 billion he is proposing to hand over to his property speculator and banker supporters is very possibly the last major tranche of taxpayers' money available to turn our economy around and he has decided to hand it over to the very same people who lined their pockets with millions during the property bubble and bankrupted the nation in the process. The government's proposals will have catastrophic consequences for our international borrowing capacity to fund a future recovery.

On 8 April 2009, Ireland finally lost its international AAA credit rating. The Irish people need to wake up to what is happening to their country, before it is too late.

Fool me once, shame on you.
Fool me twice, shame on me.

I have tried to find positive avenues along which the country could be steered towards recovery, but just as it is necessary to look at our recent past in order to avoid making the same mistakes again, it is now necessary to state clearly that our government is taking actions on a daily basis which are bringing the country ever closer to a state of ruin.

On 9 April 2009, AIB and Bank of Ireland had their international credit ratings dropped. That was two days *after* the government's announced bailout.

The government might be pulling the wool over the Irish people's eyes but the international credit rating agencies can see as clear as day what this government is up to.

The international credit agency Fitch said that while the transfers to the National Asset Management Agency should give greater certainty about the banks' asset quality and potential future impact on their profitability, this will result in an acceleration of credit losses which will exceed profits and absorb capital. As a result, Fitch believes that further capital injections on top of the combined €7 billion already received may be needed.

Fitch added that it expects further deterioration in the asset quality of residential mortgages and corporate loans books due to weaker prospects of the Irish economy and rapidly rising unemployment. The bankers are bleeding Ireland dry and will go into bankruptcy in the end anyway.

But the government can no longer say they have not been warned repeatedly from numerous reputable international sources.

Our GDP decline is accelerating. Consumer demand is contracting sharply, as evidenced by all the 'TO LET' signs on the high streets and the 70 per cent drop in car sales.

People have stopped spending, many because they are out of work, but even the people who have money are not buying because they know things will be cheaper tomorrow and next year. The economy could now be sliding into a long deflationary period, which is what can all too easily happen if we have a large, sustained drop in output. Once prices start falling, and people start to expect continuing deflation, company balance-sheet problems will become much worse than they already are and much harder to resolve, leading to more job lay-offs. This is what happened in Japan and now the same thing was also beginning to happen in Ireland. A major cause of Japan's 'lost decade' was the failure of their government to allow insolvent banks to go into bankruptcy, and Ireland's government is now charting the exact same course for its economy.

In April 2009, deflation had become a very real and present danger for Ireland.

Deflation should, or so we thought, be easy to prevent: simply increase the money supply. Large economies with free floating exchange rates – like Japan, the Eurozone, or the United States – are free to expand the money supply as much as they like. So they should find deflation easy to prevent. But it has become clear from Japan's experience, and more recently in the US and the UK, that it is not easy after all.

DEFLATION – THE KILLER BLOW

In April 2009 the slump in Irish residential housing values had already wiped out all the appreciation in household assets over the past five years. Indebted households were being forced to cut back sharply in an effort to bring their debt into line. Instead of helping the Irish people in that regard, the Irish government had decided to burden the people with even more penal taxation rates. This would further hit spending all across the economy, preventing any chance of a consumer-led economic recovery.

With car sales down 70 per cent year-on-year and the sale of goods vehicles down 77 per cent, Ireland was now staring Japanese-style deflation in the face. Cautious consumers would defer buying because of falling prices, leading to further price cuts by businesses and consequent rising unemployment.

Unless the government takes immediate action, a deep recession could very quickly become a depression. Deflation is not something many of us have experienced in our lifetime, as it last occurred in Ireland sixty years ago.

What is deflation?

Basically, deflation is when the price of a product or service will be cheaper in the future than it is today. This has the effect that people do not spend unless they absolutely have to, because if they wait things simply get cheaper. Given that a large part of our economy is driven by consumer demand, a reduction in consumer spending will have a catastrophic effect.

Adding to this problem, our consumers do not have very large savings (they had been convinced that their house was their savings), so they do not actually have much money to spend to start with. Their previous major sources of cash, which were credit cards, loans, re-financing mortgages and tax rebates, have all disappeared. Even viable businesses cannot get access to credit.

Deflation is turning out to be a serious problem for Ireland and we are going to find out that it is not as easy either to prevent or to reverse as we previously thought.

Causes of deflation

When consumers see that prices are falling and are likely to continue to fall, they have an incentive to delay their purchases. Why should they buy something now when they know it will cost much less later? This is known as a deflationary spiral.

The ultimate disaster in the current situation will be a vicious spiral of declining property prices and falling expenditure on consumption and investment. Bank losses will begin to spread from mortgages to consumer debt such as credit cards and car loans and eventually to business loans. This will result in increased levels of toxic debts for the banks. This, in turn, could lead to a disastrous economic downturn.

Increased losses and falling expenditure will begin to feed upon themselves.

Deflation usually has the effect of increasing unemployment, since the process is activated by a lower level of demand in the economy. Lower demand leads to cut-backs in production. In December 2008, Irish factory production had fallen for the tenth month in a row.

Deflation can also be brought about by a direct decline in spending, most likely through a reduction in one of the following: government spending, personal spending or investment spending.

Ireland is now suffering from a decline in all three.

The Irish banks can offer no more credit as their capital is all tied up in bad loans to insolvent builders and property speculators. A large proportion of these loans will never be repaid, but of course the bankers who issued them have already stripped out their huge bonuses for issuing the loans in the first place. They can now comfortably ride out the recession with their millions safely stashed away.

Inflation/Deflation

To understand inflation and deflation, it's necessary to understand Supply and Demand. Just like every other commodity, there is a supply of and a demand for money. Money is simply something people are willing to accept in exchange for goods or services. Price levels are the direct result of the relationship between the supply and the demand for any given item and the value of the money is subject to the same relationship.

Let's assume you are living on an island and there are ten houses for sale and a total of €1 million is available to purchase them. In that situation, you can assume that each house will cost €100,000.

If the quantity of money increases to €2 million, without increasing the quantity of houses, the price of the houses will rise to €200,000; that's inflation. If, however, the quantity of money decreases to €500,000, the price of the houses will then fall to €50,000; this is deflation.

Money supply

The money supply can be reduced if somebody on the island hoards half of it and refuses to spend it on anything. This is the second part of money supply, a reduction in spending which is bad deflation.

But what happens if you build ten more houses? You now have twenty houses and there is still only €1 million to pay for them. In that scenario, the houses once again become worth €50,000.

This is the current situation in Ireland. We have a huge surplus of housing. But the houses have not yet been fully reduced in price, because to do so would expose the bankers' past practices and sink their businesses.

There is a saying on Wall Street: 'You should never try to muscle the markets, because it's you against the world.' But the Irish bankers will twist and turn and do everything possible to avoid accepting that logic. They are currently advising the government to flood the market with money (recapitalisation) and that will fix the problem. But it won't, because Irish people know that prices will still continue to fall.

Besides, the problems with Irish banks are not ones of liquidity, but insolvency. Supply and demand determines that houses are currently overpriced by around 50 per cent and the bankers will be forced to accept this truth in the end. How much damage the banks encourage the government to inflict on the economy prior to accepting this truth is something which should be of grave concern to us all.

What's wrong with deflation?

If you don't have any debt and you can hold on to your job, then nothing. That is why the politicians, with their guaranteed incomes and gold-plated pensions are not too worried about all this; the taxpayers will pay their wages no matter how bad things get.

But the trouble is that deflation feeds on itself. Prices start slumping because there is less money available, and thus less demand. Shops have to mark down the cost of their products, profits fall and people lose their jobs. As more jobs are lost, demand keeps falling, which in turn causes more deflation. During the Great Depression of 1929, unemployment rose from 3 per cent to 25 per cent.

Deflation also makes debt more costly to service – while inflation decreases the real value of your borrowings, deflation increases it. That makes deflation very bad news for those who are heavily borrowed. Allowing things to take their course will eventually clear out bad investments made during the boom.

Politicians are very fond of telling us 'doing nothing is not an option'. But in most cases they only say this to take the focus off of themselves, the ones who created the problem in the first place. The truth is that 'doing nothing' usually is the best way forward in a deflationary cycle. Look at the United States and Japan: they have cut interest rates to zero and it makes no difference.

Quantitative easing

When they go to zero interest rates, the US Federal Reserve then begins to target the money supply. This policy is known as 'quantitative easing'. In reality, what happens is that they print more money and use this to buy Treasuries, bonds or other securities from banks to boost their reserves and get them lending again.

The Federal Reserve's balance sheet has more than doubled in size during 2008, from $915 billion to $2,200 billion. It has provided loans and emergency credits to banks, brokers and foreign countries. In January 2009, the European Central Bank (ECB) is also loaning money to Eurozone banks at 2 per cent. Unfortunately for both the Fed and the ECB, they cannot force the banks to on-lend this money. Banks are well aware that in the current recession there is going to be deflation, leading to a flood of bankruptcies (including many banks) and everybody is scared of lending. So 'quantitative easing' is not working, thus far.

In the United States, the banks are hoarding the extra money from the Fed and as a result excess reserves jumped from $2 billion in August 2008 to more than $600 billion in January 2009. But the Fed and the ECB also have the option of lending direct to governments and this money can be used for capital infrastructure projects which will create employment and hopefully get the economy going again.

The problem Ireland is experiencing is that we have so badly mismanaged our economy that even the ECB is becoming reluctant to lend us money. There is also a whiff of corruption in the air. If Ireland were a person, would you lend him/her your money? Frankly, no: Ireland looks too much like a bad loan risk.

Chapter 17

THE WAY FORWARD – WHAT TO DO?

We mentioned in the introduction to the book that restoring confidence must be a priority for this country. We suggested that business leaders must emerge of the ilk of Denis O'Brien and Michael O'Leary. To some extent, the emergence of entrepreneurs is beyond our control. We can't invent them. We can, to borrow a phrase once popular with the government, create the right conditions for business. We just need to invest phrases like that with a bit more honesty and integrity next time around. Naturally, therefore, those qualities need to be nurtured at the core of the government itself.

Government accountability

One of the first, and without any doubt the most important, issue is to establish clear accountability in the workings of government. While politicians can compel faceless civil servants to do their bidding and then protect those same civil servants from any accountability when things go wrong, we will never build a strong economy.

A good example of this, back in 2003, was when Bertie Ahern's government decided to separate the function of financial regulation from the Central Bank, by creating a new Office of the Financial Regulator, with disastrous conse-uences for the country.

Evidence has since shown that the new Regulator, Patrick Neary (a career civil servant), appeared not to have kept himself fully informed when in 2007–2008 our bankers were engaged in giving themselves millions in secret loans and shifting billions of disguised deposits between one another's banks.

Neary, in his capacity as Financial Regulator, also failed to rein in the Irish banks' reckless lending practices which led directly to the current crisis.

In an interview in May 2008, Neary said that there were signs 'we might be coming out the other end' of the liquidity crisis in the banks and criticised the rumour-mongering about Anglo Irish Bank and other Irish banks as being close to collapse. These rumours were groundless, he said.

In light of what was discovered five months later, when the government was forced to bail out the entire Irish banking system to the tune of €485 billion, that was an astonishing statement. It seems extraordinary that the Financial Regulator should be so ill-informed about the finances at Anglo Irish Bank and the other Irish banks under his control.

On 9 January 2009, Neary announced his intention to retire at the end of that month, following the completion of a report into his institution's mishandling of loans to directors at Anglo Irish Bank. Commenting on the report, Neary said he was not advised of any such issues until they were raised by the Minister for Finance in December 2008. So was this an admission that he failed to properly carry out the function of Financial Regulator?

Despite this, Neary retired with a lump sum of €428,000, equivalent to one-and-a-half times his annual salary of €5,900 per week, even though he had only been appointed to the job in 2003. He was also paid a special bonus of €202,000, equivalent to eight months' salary, in respect of the two years left on his contract. Oh, and I nearly forgot, he also got full pension rights of €2,700 per week for life, with increases equal to the pay increases granted to subsequent holders of the position of Financial Regulator, for his lifetime.

No wonder the public sector pay and pensions cost is so enormous.

The head of FÁS (the state training organisation), Roddy Molloy, who was employed by Mary Coughlan, the Minister of Enterprise, had to quit his post because of 'irregularities'.

Some of these 'irregularities' included:

€23,456 in video rentals from Xtravision, with a copy of *Legends of the Fall* incurring €3,986.45 in late fees. €19,880 for lunches in the Dublin Temple Bar restaurant Elephant (practically all of that money was accounted for by chicken wings, which the FÁS people obviously found very tasty). Can you imagine what a mountain of chicken wings you would get for twenty thousand euro?

€45,900 was spent on bottled water for staff-training sessions, each bottle costing €45. That must have been incredible water.

€90,000 was spent on an Italian Maserati car used by one of the executive's wives to bring their two children on the 600-yard journey from home to their private school. This was marked as 'necessary travel expenses'.

€75,980 was spent on a 'How to set up your own blog' training course, in which only €2,000 was spent on the actual training and the rest on hotel rooms, travel and various expenses. The reason that this portion was so expensive was because the training course was held in the Seychelles in the Indian Ocean. No point in doing it in damp, dreary Dublin, after all.

Former Taoiseach Bertie Ahern personally sanctioned the use of the government jet to fly a FÁS party to Cocoa Beach in Florida, at a total cost to the taxpayer of around €130,000. The jet, which costs €7,000 an hour to run, was used even though FÁS had also booked, and paid for, first-class airline tickets for the trip. As a result, the trip cost the taxpayer around €80,000 to fly the seven delegates via private jet, and a further €4,824 per head was given to a commercial airline for first class tickets. FÁS said that they had forgotten to cancel the extra tickets. They also said the first class flights were booked, just in case the then Taoiseach would need the state's private jet at short notice. A spokesperson for Minister Mary Harney insisted that the Taoiseach of the time, Bertie Ahern, would have personally approved its use by the FÁS junketeers. 'The matter of the government jet is entirely a matter for the Taoiseach,' the spokesperson said.

FÁS staff also carried credit cards which had limits of €76,000.

THE WAY FORWARD – WHAT TO DO?

But when the head of FÁS, Roddy Molloy, (also a career civil servant) from Birr in County Offlay (Brian Cowen's constituency), was forced to 'retire' as a result of these revelations, he did so in style, walking away with a lump sum of nearly half a million *and* full pension entitlements.

Taoiseach Brian Cowen said at the time that Molloy's severance arrangements would be made 'in line with public sector norms. That's the normal procedure, and he will have that entitlement the same as everybody else in that position.'

Cowen, a personal friend of Roddy Molloy's, expressed his full confidence in the man he described as 'an excellent public servant'. In June 2008, Cowen also defended Molloy in the Dáil saying that he was 'a person whom I personally hold in the highest regard'.

Brian Cowen obviously had no problem with how FÁS misspent a massive €5.7 million of taxpayer's money on travel and other expenses in 2007.

It is very difficult to get good performance in government if civil servants can do an absolutely terrible job, be forced to resign and then suffer no penalty. In the private sector you would be sacked on the grounds of incompetence (unless of course you were a senior executive at a large bank).

But the public sector is protected by law in that regard. For example, the bulk of Patrick Neary's golden handshake related to his pension entitlements, which are thus protected. In the 1990s, the Supreme and High Courts refused to allow the pensions of two state employees to be forfeited despite their convictions for criminal offences.

In 1991, the Supreme Court struck down provisions of the Offences Against the State Act,1939, which provided that whenever anyone employed by the state or local authorities was convicted by the Special Criminal Court, they would lose their job and any pension entitlements in addition to whatever other penalty was imposed by the court.

In 1988, Thomas Cox, a former schoolteacher, was jailed for possessing arms and he claimed that his personal rights were infringed by the anti-terror rule. The Supreme Court found that the ban was a disproportionate violation of Cox's property rights and right to earn a livelihood.

So, even if Patrick Neary had been fired for gross incompetence, his pension would have been protected. In relation to his lump sum of €428,000, Neary was able to protect this by being allowed to retire and thereby avoid financial penalties for being fired and leaving his job in disgrace. Laws need to be changed in this whole area, by referendum if necessary, if we are to have any possibility of good, transparent, accountable government in future. If we fail to do so, we are destined to repeat past mistakes, with further disastrous consequences for the country.

But does the government believe that lack of accountability in these areas is a problem?

Acknowledging the poor reputation of Ireland abroad, Lenihan said that steps would be taken to plot a course for the economy over the coming years. 'People are saying different things about Ireland around the world and there is a very negative message about our financial services,' said Lenihan. 'I think it is important to reassure that we are determined to repair the damage that has been done to our reputation and image through what did happen at one particular bank.' From that statement it appears that the

Minister sees government accountability as having nothing whatsoever to do with the recent scandals in the financial sector, or am I missing something?

The Irish banks

We need to appoint some seasoned independent international bankers (from other EU countries if necessary) to the Central Bank board and other key fiscal and regulatory positions.

For the past two decades, both monetary policy and financial regulation in Ireland has been dominated by career civil servants and other political appointees, the majority of whom knew nothing about financial markets, or if they did they were in some way beholden to the industry they were appointed to police.

This will have to rectified if we are to successfully rebuild our financial services sector. The government should also require the registration of all securities sold to the public and to pension funds and compel banks and other financial institutions to trade these on the Irish Stock Exchange, where there can be proper transparency, disclosure and regulation.

We need to impose greater personal and market discipline, with crystal-clear transparency on banks and bankers. Selling securities/bonds that are designed to be misleading and defraud investors should be made a criminal offence and those responsible for such acts should face prison terms of five years.

In the words of Bo Lündgren, Director General of Sweden's national debt office: 'Legislation should be introduced so that bank executives responsible for reckless lending would be punished under criminal law, or be forced to pay damages.'

In 2009, Irish banks no longer existed because of their capital reserves and assets, but on the charity of the Irish taxpayers, and they should not be allowed to forget it. They sacrificed all independence when they required Irish taxpayers to become liable for their gambling debts. Although the complaisance of government authorities towards them would sometimes make you wonder.

Restoring confidence in the banking system is now a major priority for the government, but the days of the banks calling the shots will have to end.

Proper regulation, unannounced spot checks, absolute transparency and no guff about withholding 'commercially sensitive information' is what is required.

Only then will confidence be restored.

Chapter 18

ABANDON THE EURO – SHOULD WE?

Many people have told me that 'Ireland would be at a huge disadvantage if it were not part of European Monetary Union (EMU) and in the Eurozone'.

They say American companies would no longer want to invest here.

So then I ask: 'What other reasons are there for staying part of the Eurozone?' In reply, most people have very little else to say about the subject, except that they seem convinced that it's vitally important that we stay in. But is that really true?

If we did opt out, we would be still be part of the European Union, we would just not be part of the EU monetary system. Sweden, the UK and Denmark are all outside the Eurozone and they seem to be managing very well.

There are lots of ways in which converting from the punt to the euro has not been a fantastic success for Ireland.

Remember the huge price increases in the shops immediately after joining the euro, and when we asked the then Minister Harney to introduce price controls she famously told us to 'shop around'.

Jean-Claude Trichet, President of the European Central Bank (ECB), wrongly delayed by a year in cutting interest rates, telling us all through 2008 that inflation was going to get completely out of hand in the Eurozone countries. This had the effect of pushing up the value of the euro against sterling and pricing Irish exports out of the UK market, one of our main trading partners. Then, in early 2009, Trichet did an about-face and said there was no credible deflation facing these countries.

'There is presently no threat of deflation,' Trichet told a committee of the European Parliament on 14 February 2009. 'We are currently witnessing a process of disinflation, driven in particular by a sharp decline in commodity prices. It is a welcome development,' he added.

This illustrated a spectacular lack of economic judgment, considering that Eurozone inflation was already, at that stage, significantly undershooting the European Central Bank's own target (and principle policy objective) of maintaining the annual rate *below but close* to 2 per cent. In fact, in February 2009 the rate of consumer price inflation in the Eurozone was heading straight into negative territory and deflation was looming large.

In February 2009, we in Ireland did not need President Trichet to tell us that deflation, or *'disinflation'* as he liked to call it, was about to hit the economy, because everybody knew at that stage it had already arrived. House prices were falling fast, car prices were falling and wages were falling. In the spring of 2009, the only things on the increase in Ireland were bad debts, the numbers of unemployed, massive golden handshakes to civil servants who were resigning in disgrace and huge increases in politicians' budgets for spin-doctoring.

Trichet was spectacularly wrong on inflation, then on deflation and the need to cut interest rates.

Was it really in Ireland's best interests to be pegged to a currency which had someone like this, who was wrong all the time, determining our interest rates?

The very clear and definite answer has to be NO!

In the eight years, 1993–2000, Ireland had a growth rate averaging 7 per cent a year. The most important single reason for this period of economic growth was the fact that we devalued our currency by 10 per cent in 1993 and allowed our currency to float against the currencies of our principal trading partners. This gave Ireland a very competitive exchange rate, which boosted exports, helped keep out imports and led to a high rate of economic growth and output.

At the time, politicians of all parties and most economists were opposed to joining the Eurozone without the UK being in it also. They finally went ahead in the belief that the UK would join inside a year or two.

Irish export figures January–November 2008
                    € (in millions)
Total worldwide   **79,873**
Total Eurozone   **32,286**
Total outside Eurozone   **47,587**

Irish import figures January–November 2008
                    € (in millions)
Total worldwide   **52,794**
Total Eurozone   **13,453**
Total outside Eurozone   **39,341**

Ireland conducts the vast majority of its trade with countries outside the Eurozone. By joining the euro, we tied our currency to an area with which we do only a minority of our trade, while the countries with which we do the majority of our trade have the freedom to pursue independent exchange rate and interest rate policies.

When we joined EMU we abandoned any independent control over our currency exchange rate or interest rate, despite the undoubted importance of these to an economy like ours which depends so much on exports. We ended up with a situation where unsustainable interest rates were being imposed upon us by the European Central Bank in Frankfurt. So, when we needed higher interest rates in 2003–2004, we were powerless to change them and ended up in the current mess.

If the Irish Central Bank had retained its independence, instead of surrendering it on joining the Eurozone, it would undoubtedly have raised Irish interest rates during this period to lower economic growth and inflation of asset prices. But Germany and France wanted lower interest rates and we were caught in the middle.

By February 2009, Ireland had a budget deficit of 9 per cent of GDP, the highest in the Eurozone.

When Ireland joined the euro we agreed to keep borrowings to 3 per cent of GDP. In the spring of 2009 we were already over 10 per cent, and rising, so it was only a matter of time until we got pushed out of the euro anyway.

It was always going to be very difficult for sixteen separate countries with widely differing economic performances, languages, legal frameworks, labour laws and tax regimes to make a success of the EMU.

By the spring of 2009, more and more Irish people were starting to face facts and admit that it was not in their best interests to be part of the Eurozone. Tying Ireland's currency to that of a strong country like Germany was just not sustainable. Also in the spring of 2009, many people in Ireland were of the belief that the Germans would bail us out, although they never gave any plausible reason as to why they thought this might happen.

Besides, the Maastricht Treaty, at the insistence of Germany, actually forbids it.

The reality in 2009 was that Germany was looking east to the new accession states of Poland, Hungary, the Czech and Slovak Republics, Romania, Bulgaria and the Baltic States, as these are Germany's future exports markets. These were the economies Germany was going to help and not Ireland. The Germans also held the view that Ireland had a very weak economy, built largely on EU aid and low corporation tax.

The following is a very unpalatable truth to have to hear: in September 2007, there was a gathering of eighty German industrialists at Clontarf Castle in Dublin. These were members of the German Federation of Buying and Marketing Groups, representing potential investors in Ireland. The meeting was addressed by the German Ambassador to Dublin, Christian Pauls.

The Ambassador's address was in German and we only learned about it because an Irish Member of the European Parliament, Gay Mitchell, was present and the address was translated for him as he was due to speak next. Pauls said: 'Ireland is a coarse place with a sad history where the natives are obsessed by money.' He criticised Ireland's recent affluence and said 'its Government had junior ministers earning more than the German Chancellor' and that '20 per cent of the population are public servants'. He described the country's health service as chaotic, with hospital waiting lists which would not be tolerated anywhere else in the world.

He said he was astonished to learn that Irish doctors who were offered annual salaries of €200,000 to work in the public sector turned their noses up at what they called 'Mickey Mouse money'. He went on to describe Irish history as 'even sadder than Poland'. Dermot Gallagher, the Secretary-General of the Department of Foreign Affairs, was instructed by Foreign Minister Dermot Ahern, to lodge a formal protest. Reinod Herber, a spokesman for the German Embassy, said: 'Maybe he misjudged the humour. I don't think he tried to insult the Irish people. My Ambassador is a humorous man and maybe that humour was misunderstood.'

However accurate or otherwise Pauls' comments were, that was the official German government view of Ireland in September 2007. Why, then, would people expect such a country to come to our aid eighteen months later when our economy lay in ruins?

It should also be pointed out that the German Ambassador's talk was against the backdrop of Ireland's Taoiseach Bertie Ahern giving testimony to a tribunal in Dublin Castle. On the previous Friday afternoon, 12 September 2007, Ahern was booed by members of the public as he left the tribunal. A few months later, Bertie Ahern was no longer Taoiseach and was replaced by his Finance Minister, Brian Cowen.

We should always have confidence in our own abilities and one of the major benefits of the Celtic Tiger years was the look of confidence one saw on the faces of Ireland's young people. But we should not let that confidence cloud our perception of ourselves as being a unique race of people who are loved and respected by the whole world. While we may not be exactly loved by the whole world it is true to say that we don't have too many enemies; but in relation to respect, that is something which has to be earned.

The Irish people need to realise that we are caught in a snare created by the vices of greedy men and we will have to free ourselves by dint of own own decisions and courage and not be relying on Germany, or anybody else, for charity.

At the end of 2008, a Eurozone country leaving the euro was close to an unthinkable event. But in January 2009, when the credit rating agency Standard & Poor's down-graded its outlook for Ireland, from stable to negative and warned that the country could lose its 'AAA' sovereign credit rating (which it did) if the government's attempts to boost the economy failed to improve growth prospects, it left many thinking the unthinkable. The huge exposure, €485 billion, to the banks that the Irish government had taken on in September 2008 was now beginning to have a serious impact on Ireland's creditworthiness. Such deterioration in the state's credit rating would further increase the cost of borrowing for the government.

All the fiscal rectitude in the world will not save the Irish economy if any significant portion of that bank guarantee were to be exercised.

Chapter 19

DEVALUATION – WOULD IT HELP?

P rior to Ireland joining European Monetary Union (EMU), Kevin O'Rourke, Professor of Economics at Trinity College Dublin, believed that joining EMU and losing the power to devalue the punt was risky. He saw devaluation as an easier way to reduce wage costs than doing it in a more explicit fashion. Without the devaluation tool, the only way the government can solve the budgetary problem is to raise taxes and cut expenditure, which will lead to increased job losses.

Although some economists are reluctant to admit it, devaluation does work. It works by cutting the value of workers' wages, rather than by reducing the amount they see on their payslip every week and it does this by making the currency they are being paid in less valuable. But this only becomes apparent if they buy imported goods. The result is less expensive labour, which in turn helps to reduce the price of our exports and therefore increase sales and create more employment. It makes the remedial economic medicine easier to swallow, because workers in export-orientated industries know that it will help to protect existing jobs and create new jobs as the economy recovers.

If devaluation is not an option then real wages have to fall if Ireland is to regain its competitiveness.

In the spring of 2009 we began to see how difficult this was going to be, especially in relation to the public sector, whose pay and pension entitlements were consuming over half of all government income.

Public sector pay and pensions bill = €20 billion, government income €34 billion.

In the private sector, some firms were simply closing down rather than go through the almost impossible task of getting unions to accept pay cuts for their members.

If we decided to devalue, laws would have to be passed and new notes and coins would have to be produced. International investors would know the reason we were doing this was because we were going to devalue the currency, so they would remove their deposits from Irish banks until this had been done. There is no doubt that there would be pain associated with devaluation. But devaluation would allow us to avoid mass unemployment.

It is inevitable that there would be a price to pay for re-establishing control over our currency, our interest rates and our economic destiny. But it would be a price worth paying. Many commentators will advise the government: 'You can't devalue, because the Irish private sector has a lot of debts in euros and devaluation would make it very hard for those borrowers to service those debts.' But, of course, the alternative – sharp wage cuts, causing major domestic deflation – would also make it hard to service those debts.

The only other solution is to drastically cut public sector pay and pensions, by about 20 per cent, across the board and allow President of the European Central Bank, Jean-Claude Trichet, to continue to have control of our economic future.

In the absence of devaluation, there is therefore no alternative to wage reductions, because our wages are too high relative to our productivity levels, and relative to wages abroad. Unfortunately, these wage reductions will have to come very quickly, and painfully, if we are to have any chance of arresting the number of jobs being lost on a weekly basis.

Ireland lost 9,000 jobs per week in January 2009. There was a big furore in December 2008 when the computer company Dell cut 2,000 jobs in Limerick, but one month later Ireland was losing the equivalent of more than four Dells per week, or over a thousand jobs a day.

The unprotected private sector will be taken care of by market forces. This was evident by the spring of 2009 when a third of a million private sector workers found themselves out of work and this figure was definitely heading for half a million by year's end.

In the past, emigration was always a safety valve for the private sector, but in 2009 this was not as easy an option as it had been previously, because unemployment was rising in countries like America, the UK and Australia, which were the traditional destinations of Irish emigrants.

Aside from the human devastation caused by hundreds of thousands of people finding themselves out of work there is also a huge cost to the government. In March 2009, the Labour Minister, Mary Hanafin, said that each 100,000 out of work was costing the country €1.3 billion per year. So, in March 2009 with the unemployed figure at around 350,000, the annual cost to the government was €4.55 billion and when the number rises to 500,000 unemployed (as predicted for the year end) this figure will be €6.5 billion. This, on top of a public sector pay and pensions bill of €20 billion per annum, will break the country.

The Irish economy was coming very close to its tipping point.

The government was staring economic collapse in the face unless it moved very quickly to reduce costs and halt the slide in unemployment. They were simply going to run out of money. In the absence of deep cuts in the public sector pay and pensions bill, there was no relief on the horizon; which meant that there was nothing to give the economic quick-fix necessary to arrest the country's decline – unless the option of devaluation could somehow be exercised.

Currency devaluation has the ability to very quickly stimulate exports, create employment, revive the economy and its benefits far outweigh any disadvantages.

These benefits would not happen overnight, it would take about two years to take effect fully. But at least we would be correctly positioned when the world economies began to turn around in 2011.

Any other course of action would simply be wishful thinking.

To achieve devaluation we would have to abandon the euro and tie our currency to either the UK pound, or the US dollar. In 1993, Ireland had been forced to devalue by 10 per cent, largely because of a loss of competitiveness resulting from the huge devaluation by Britain, our major trading partner. Devaluation had been very successful on that occasion.

In 2009, Irish firms had once again been priced out of the UK market, this time by the appreciation of the euro against sterling, as a result of the Bank of England drastically cutting interest rates and the European Central Bank delaying comparable action. Similarly, the euro had also risen in value against the dollar.

At the beginning of 2009, with the fall in Irish consumer purchasing power and tax revenues declining rapidly, exports were the last remaining engine driving Ireland's economy and devaluation would be the only way to boost those.

Devaluation can only be avoided if the government can reverse the situation whereby the public sector is consuming over half the annual income of the government. But in early 2009 it did not look like the Irish government was capable of facing up to that task.

Raising taxes seemed to be their preferred option to balance the books and any fool could see that this course of action would only accelerate the economic decline.

The government had made a disastrous mistake back in 2003–2004 when they failed to heed Charlie McCreevy's advice to rein in the economy and they were now about to compound that mistake in 2009.

There is, of course, one other option to politicians who in times like these want to sidestep their responsibility for taking difficult decisions: they can threaten to throw the country to the mercy of the dreaded IMF (International

Monetary Fund) and propose to let them make the hard decisions. In January 2009, Hungary had arranged an IMF-led rescue loan of €20 billion and the IMF insisted on an immediate across-the-board, public sector wage cut of 8 per cent as one of its conditions.

Ireland should cut its public sector debt, abandon the euro, peg itself to the dollar, devalue its currency, boost exports, attract inward investment and put its people back to work.

We should also reduce the debt value of home owners; this would put liquidity directly into people's pockets and boost consumer spending, which would take effect prior to our exports getting going again.

This would be a much better use of government funds than shovelling billions into banks who will only use the money to deflate their toxic balance sheets.

All these banks have more debt liabilities than assets and do not have any capital, so they are all entirely insolvent.

Where would Ireland find the money to stimulate the economy? As mentioned in the introduction to this book, Ireland currently has about €300 billion in deposits. The government could create a national recovery bond and ensure that it was attractive enough to attract investment. Raising taxes in the belief that this would create capital would simply be the final nail in the economic coffin. But then, we have come to accept government stupidity as normal.

Chapter 20

ENERGY SUPPLY SECURITY

Wherever we look upon this earth,
the opportunities take shape within the problems.
Nelson A. Rockefeller

F ixing our banking system, regaining control of our currency, providing accountable and transparent government, creating a realistic public sector pay and pensions regime and putting our people back to work – these are all necessary steps if we are to rebuild our shattered economy, but putting in place an affordable and secure energy supply for Ireland is as important for Ireland's future as all these put together. It is not an exaggeration to say that Ireland's future prosperity depends on how successfully we manage this very important task.

Securing a reliable and affordable supply of energy; and effecting a rapid transformation to a low-carbon, efficient and environmentally benign system of energy supply will require imagination and courage. What is needed is nothing short of an energy revolution.

As a young idealistic Irishman, I campaigned for Jimmy Carter in the New York Democratic Party in the spring of 1976 and had the pleasure of meeting him at the Democratic National Convention in Madison Square Garden on 15 July of that year. On 18 April 1977 he made a speech entitled 'The President's Proposed Energy Policy.'

> Tonight I want to have an unpleasant talk with you about a problem unprecedented in our history. With the exception of preventing war, this is the greatest challenge our country will face during our lifetimes. The energy crisis has not yet overwhelmed us, but it will if we do not act quickly.
>
> It is a problem we will not solve in the next few years, and it is likely to get progressively worse through the rest of this century. We must not be selfish or timid if we hope to have a decent world for our children and grandchildren. We simply must balance our demand for energy with our rapidly shrinking resources. By acting now, we can control our future instead of letting the future control us . . . Our decision about energy will test the character of the American people and the ability of the President and the Congress to govern. This difficult effort will be the 'moral equivalent of war,' except that we will be uniting our efforts to build and not destroy . . . The world has not prepared for the future. During the 1950s, people used twice as much oil as during the 1940s. During the 1960s, we used

twice as much as during the 1950s. And in each of those decades, more oil was consumed than in all of mankind's previous history . . .

Ours is the most wasteful nation on earth. We waste more energy than we import. With about the same standard of living, we use twice as much energy per person as do other countries like Germany, Japan and Sweden.

One choice is to continue doing what we have been doing before. We can drift along for a few more years. We can delay insulating our houses, and they will continue to lose about fifty per cent of their heat in waste. We can continue using scarce oil and natural resources to generate electricity, and continue wasting two-thirds of their fuel value in the process . . . But we still have another choice. We can begin to prepare right now. We can decide to act while there is time . . . Only by saving energy can we maintain our standard of living and keep our people at work . . .

I believe this can be a positive challenge . . . We have always wanted to give our children and grand-children a world richer in possibilities than we've had. They are the ones we must provide for now. They are the ones who will suffer most if we don't act.

Jimmy Carter's description of America's need to confront the issue of secure energy supplies as being 'the moral equivalent of war' is exactly the position Ireland now needs to adopt in ensuring our future energy supply security.

Without clean, affordable, energy sources, Ireland will become caught in a 'development trap': we will be forced to either sacrifice our climate and ecological security in the name of economic development or condemn our citizens to poverty in the name of climate protection.

We urgently need to decarbonise the energy we use and provide access to an ample and affordable energy supply with which to power our economic prosperity in the decades ahead.

We are now at a crossroads in this regard and Ireland's current energy trends are unsustainable environmentally and socially; but there is time to change the road we are on. Up to now we have consistently and significantly underestimated our greenhouse gas emission predictions. Increased levels of greenhouse gases in the atmosphere – primarily carbon dioxide, methane, nitrous oxide, and chlorofluorocarbons – are linked with the global phenomenon of climate change. Slowing the growth in greenhouse gas emissions, while ensuring availability of the plentiful energy essential to economic vitality is a major challenge for all Irish people and we need to act fast.

Throughout the past decade, our nation's extraordinary development was fuelled, in large part, by fossil energy. Looking toward the future, we must now discover how best to ensure secure, reliable, and affordable alternative energy supplies for the coming decades.

Despite gains which can be made in energy efficiency, Ireland will require increased energy supplies in the next twenty years to fuel a growing economy.

Aside from environmental concerns, growth in demand for fossil fuels in developing economies such as China and India is going to significantly increase in the years ahead, and this will pose a direct threat to Ireland's energy security and development as it will drive up prices and squeeze supplies. Ireland's task now is to plan ahead and avoid being caught in this squeeze, when it inevitably occurs.

It used to be commonly held that economic growth was inescapably linked to higher energy consumption and thus more greenhouse gas emissions. Cutting emissions, therefore, tends to be seen as contrary to economic growth. Out of necessity this view is now changing. Most governments agree to combat climate change by reducing greenhouse gas emissions, but the central question is: will we have to sacrifice economic growth to do it?

Accumulating evidence shows that it is possible to pursue economic expansion and at the same time stabilise energy consumption and safeguard the environment.

'The Stern Review on the Economics of Climate Change' is a 700-page report released in October 2006 by economist Lord Stern of Brentford for the British government. It discusses the effect of climate change and global warming on the world economy.

Although not the first economic report on global warming, it is significant as the largest and most widely known and discussed report of its kind. The Stern Report concluded that the global costs of stabilising the climate are significant, but manageable. The costs are limited to around 1 per cent of global GDP each year.

In contrast, the report estimates that if we do not act, the overall costs and risks of climate change will be equivalent to losing at least 5 per cent of global GDP each year. Ireland, therefore, cannot afford not to act – and act decisively.

The fight against global warming involves us all, from our largest business organisations, to local communities and private individuals. It is a collective challenge in which every one of us has a role.

Energy use by households accounts for not only a large share of Ireland's total energy consumption, but often also a significant share of energy wasted. Reducing this wastage could make an important contribution to reducing CO_2 emissions. In Ireland, prevention of energy waste in households needs to become a government focus. The government needs to introduce a range of energy-saving policy initiatives together with building regulations designed to help householders reduce energy consumption (and thus energy bills) and minimise the environmental impact. Insulation and tighter-sealing doors and windows can lower heating bills significantly.

The Building Energy Rating (BER) scheme, now in force, is an important step to achieving energy savings in buildings, both existing and new. Both retailer and consumer incentives need to be introduced and promoted in this area. There are huge business opportunities here in insulation materials for roofs, walls and floors, energy monitoring and thermostat control systems.

These new business opportunities will create thousands of new 'green jobs'. Irish architects and engineers can build up exportable services in these fields. Such companies can market their services at international trade fairs, focusing on sustainable building solutions.

Ireland needs to formulate a long-term energy policy to ensure a balance between security of supply, economic growth and respect for the environment. This should be a plan extending out to 2025. It should put forward a range of initiatives that look at energy security from both the consumption and production perspective: intensified energy-saving efforts to reduce overall energy consumption; increased use of renewable energy to reduce reliance on fossil fuels and an intensified focus on more effective technologies and alternative fuels to provide competitive alternatives to diesel and gasoline in the transport sector.

This again creates business opportunities and 'green jobs'.

> *Our greatest glory consists not in never falling,*
> *but in rising every time we fall.*
> **Oliver Goldsmith**

The Irish government should now enter into a broad cross-party near-term energy agreement. This agreement should lay down Ireland's energy policy for 2009–2012, which meets or surpasses EU environmental goals in several areas. The energy policy should demonstrate Ireland's commitment to responsible energy use.

Action is needed everywhere. It must permeate our entire society, from the way in which we build houses, how we light our homes, where the heat in the radiator comes from and whether cars run on renewable fuels or old fashioned petrol. It has importance for industry, for institutions and for every citizen. The energy agreement should include the establishment of new offshore wind farms generating clean electricity, tax-exempting electric cars and cars fuelled by hydrogen up to 2012 and the provision of state funding for research into electric vehicles, solar energy, algae biofuels, hydrogen fuel cells, wave power and any other technology that looks promising.

The agreement should illustrate that today, secure energy supplies are of critical importance to the future well-being of the Irish economy and the Irish people.

Chapter 21

GREEN ENERGY TECHNOLOGIES AND OPPORTUNITIES

The EU commission has set targets to substitute 5.75 per cent of fossil fuels with biofuels by 2010.

Environmental technology (EnviroTech), Green technology (GreenTech) and Clean technology (CleanTech), call it what you will, is a commercial market with incredible future opportunities. The worldwide energy market is estimated at $5 trillion annually, that is $5,000,000,000,000 or five million, million dollars. If just 1 per cent of this enormous market goes over to green energy in the next five years, that's an entirely new commercial market worth $50 billion per year. This has to be one of the greatest economic opportunities of the twenty-first century.

Investment in new technologies, equipment, buildings, and infrastructure could provide a stimulus for much-needed new Irish business and employment opportunities. The employment potential in renewable energy and supplier industries will see rapid expansion in the years ahead.

The whole area of biofuels has enormous potential for Ireland, if for no other reason than that there is an import replacement market worth €6 billion (current imported fuels bill) per annum already in existence. If Irish businesses could capture 5 per cent of this indigenous market per year they would have a whole new industry worth €300 million in year one and which could grow at the rate of 100 per cent per annum for twenty years, until it was eventually worth €6 billion per annum, in today's money. What other industry offers the Irish economy an opportunity of that magnitude? And that's just the biofuels sector; then there is solar, wind, wave, geothermal and nuclear.

The possibilities are simply enormous.

> *Times of great calamity and confusion have ever been productive of the greatest minds. The purest ore is produced from the hottest furnace, and the brightest thunderbolt is elicited from the darkest storm.*
>
> **Charles Caleb Colton**

To get this industry rapidly off the ground will require government involvement with subsidies, pro-green-tech policies and a decision to purchase the kinds of fuels and technologies these start-ups will be marketing. This will also greatly assist in getting early-stage venture capitalists interested.

But no amount of money will matter without government policies that foster a market for alternative sources of energy and energy-efficient products. The international political winds have shifted rapidly toward green technology and Ireland should become part of this movement. The government should consider setting up a green-tech renewable energy research and development organisation and have it take a leadership role in clean energy research, development and deployment, by designing technologies that will allow Ireland to enjoy a growing, prosperous economy while reducing greenhouse gas emissions.

The government should also consider instituting loan guarantees to help new green-tech companies get off the ground. It is essential that we create a strong, predictable market for energy innovations with concrete goals that will speed the introduction of innovative products and provide a strong incentive for private R&D investment in energy technologies.

The economy is currently getting everyone's attention and, while 'technology policy' may not yet be a topic of everyday conversation, the government should be creating plans to make Green Energy technology a national priority.

Ireland needs to make renewable energy sources the dominant feature of our energy system, and systematically phase out reliance on fossil fuels. Ireland has huge potential in the renewable energy field, an industry which associates well with Ireland's 'green' brand. The pursuit of so-called 'green jobs' employment – which will also contribute to protecting the environment and reducing carbon emissions – can be a key economic driver for Ireland in the next decade. Construction jobs can be greened by ensuring that new buildings meet high energy-performance standards.

Retrofitting existing buildings to make them more energy-efficient has large job creation potential for construction workers, architects, energy auditors, engineers, and others.

The potential for green jobs is very significant. But much of it will not materialise without sustained investment by both the public and private sectors. The government needs to establish a firm framework for greening all aspects of the economy, with the help of targets and directives, business incentives, and reformed taxation and subsidy policies. Co-operative technology development and technology-sharing programmes could help expedite developments in these areas.

We also need to provide as many workers as possible with the qualifications which will increasingly be needed; an expansion of green education, training, and skill-building programmes in a broad range of occupations will be necessary. In future, renewable energy sources will provide a superior alternative to burning fossil fuels and it is essential to start using them now in order to gain necessary experience.

A recent report entitled 'The Atlantic Century: Benchmarking EU and US Innovation and Competitiveness,' was produced by think-tank and education-institute the Information Technology and Innovation Foundation in Washington DC. The report comprehensively evaluated Europe and the Unites States on innovation and competitiveness, covering forty countries. It ranked countries and regions on the basis of how much they have changed, improved or slipped, over a decade in each of the various categories. Ireland was placed thirteenth overall which means that it lags behind Singapore at 1, Sweden at 2, Luxembourg at 3, Denmark at 4, Finland at 7, Britain at 8, the Netherlands at 11 and France at 12 and the US comes in at 6.

The report indicates that all other thirty-nine countries and regions considered in the study are moving more rapidly towards a knowledge-based innovation economy than the US (another depressing legacy of the Bush administration). The report says Europe will overtake the US in just over a decade if the situation remains static. 'If the EU-15 region as a whole continues to improve at this faster rate than the United States, it would surpass the United States in innovation-based competitiveness by 2020,' it said.

Overall, Ireland was placed seventh for entrepreneurship. But it was ranked eighteenth in the key category of R&D, with the report's authors noting: 'In spite of Ireland's economic progress, that country is actually very far behind in government R&D, only barely ahead of China, and actually below the EU-10 (the accession countries).'

Ireland also only comes in fifteenth overall for its current Internet broadband infrastructure. Ireland does well in the category of 'ease of doing business' (ranked fourth), for its trade balance, exports set against imports, (ranked third), and in the numbers who attain higher education (ranked fifth).

While Ireland does relatively poorly compared to the US in the number of researchers employed per capita (ranking fourteenth overall), it does better than Britain at sixteenth place.

In the most important area of 'availability of venture capital,' Ireland only comes in thirteenth in the report. This represents a worrying 40 per cent decline in potential funding between 2000 and 2006.

Venture capital is the lifeblood of R&D and the government will need to increase dramatically the attractiveness and tax efficiency of investing in this whole area.

If each 100,000 people unemployed costs the Irish government €1.3 billion and there is €300 billion on deposit in Irish banks, would it not make sense for the government to float a Green Technology Innovation Bond, which would have very generous tax benefits? The bond could be for €1 billion, which could then be leveraged to €5 billion and it could be jointly managed by the Treasury Management Agency and the IDA.

Renewable energy sources are mostly cost-free commodities to which everyone has unlimited access. Ireland has at its disposal a range of different renewable energy sources, but with the exception of wind and hydropower, these have barely been exploited.

Hydropower

When we normally think of hydropower, we immediately think of dams and turbines and in that regard it is safe to say that the potential for hydropower in Ireland has almost been exploited to its full extent. But there is now a new hydro technology called 'hydrokinetics'. Traditional hydropower harvests the potential energy of falling water. Hydrokinetic technology reaps energy from water as it moves laterally, either in the flow of a river or in the change of tides. So far, the designs are very diverse and it is an early-stage technology.

Commercial installations are mounted on the seabed
(courtesy of OpenHydro Group Ltd).

Some companies are developing helical turbines; some are working on turbines that are wheel-shaped. Several companies are taking advantage of a hydrofoil-type principle and some are carrying out R&D on what looks like a wind turbine adjusted to work underwater. Its blades are shorter and thicker than wind turbines and the rotor faces downstream of the current, instead of upwind. 'Hydrokinetics' now, is where wind was thirty years ago.

One of the advantages of hydrokinetics is that because most cities have a body of water flowing through them, power generation can be closer to the people who use it. Less energy is wasted in transmission, freeing up more for consumers.

One of the main obstacles to be overcome at present is finding blade material strong enough to work in a medium that is 800 times denser than air.

No one knows what impact these turbines will have on fish and other river life, particularly migrating salmon, so they are probably going to be better suited to marine sites.

An Irish renewable engineering company, OpenHydro, has come up with innovative technology in this area. They have developed what they call an Open-Centre Turbine which is designed to be deployed directly on the seabed.

Installations will be silent and invisible from the surface. They will be located at depth and present no navigational hazard. Farms of Open-Centre Turbines will provide a significant and undetectable supply of clean, predictable, renewable energy.

Communities that benefit from power supplied by Open-Centre Turbine technology will never be conscious of the turbines' existence.

In October 2008, OpenHydro announced that it had been selected by Électricité de France (EDF) to develop the first tidal current farm to be connected to the French electricity grid.

The project involves the installation of ten large seabed-mounted marine turbines in a tidal farm located in the Paimpol-Bréhat (Côtes d'Armor) region of Brittany. The project is expected to create up to thirty new jobs at OpenHydro's manufacturing facility at Greenore, County Louth. OpenHydro's technology converts the movement of water in tidal streams directly into electricity.

Advantages of generating electricity using the Open-Centre turbine technology include:

- The electricity produced is completely renewable since it relies on tidal currents that are created by the gravitational effect of the sun and moon on the world's oceans.
- Whereas other forms of renewable energy are dependent on the weather conditions that day (e.g., the amount of wind or a clear sky), tidal energy is completely predictable, giving the electricity produced a premium value.
- Since the turbines are located beneath the surface, they are protected from storm damage and cannot be seen or heard. The design is considered to have no impact on marine mammals since it has no oils which can leak, no exposed blade tips and a significant opening at its centre.
- Due to the density of water, a relatively small turbine can produce the same power as a much larger wind turbine.

OpenHydro is a clear demonstration of how Irish companies can very quickly become world leaders in the field of 'Green Energy'.

Pierre Gadonneix, Chairman and Chief Executive, EDF, said: 'This project places EDF and France among the world leaders in marine energy and is part of our respective commitments in the fight against global warming. While the EDF Group's commitment in this sector is long standing – the tidal power station at La Rance, built over forty years ago, remains the most powerful one in the world – it is also involved in numerous projects through its subsidiaries, EDF Energy and EDF Energies Nouvelles.'

OpenHydro became the first company to deploy a free-standing tidal turbine directly onto the seabed at the European Marine Energy Centre (EMEC) in Orkney, Scotland.

OpenHydro has secured shareholder funding of €50 million since 2005 for the commercial development of its turbines.

Wind energy

Wind energy is one of the cleanest ways to generate electricity and it produces neither emissions nor toxic waste. The Irish potential offered by wind power systems is very significant. Our off-shore potential in particular can play a major role in future electricity generation.

A large increase in wind power fed into the grid will make adjustments in grid management necessary.

In 2008, the ESB announced plans to build a €40-million wind farm near Six-mile-cross in County Tyrone. It also announced a €22-billion investment plan, €11 billion of which will be invested in renewable energy. That is a very significant pool of cash which should be utilised in kick-starting Ireland's new green energy industries.

Irish energy entrepreneur Eddie O'Connor is a world leader in the field of wind power. He founded the international wind energy company Airtricity in 1999. Back in 1997 he began searching across Ireland for wind-farm sites with just €625,000 in equity backing before establishing Future Wind Partnership and subsequently Airtricity. In April 2007, Airtricity entered into an €800-million joint venture to develop 600 megawatts of onshore wind farm projects in Portugal. The turbines alone will cost around €600 million, with labour and land access rights making up most of the rest. At the time, O'Connor said; 'We are proud to be able to help Portugal to reach its ambitious target of forty-five per cent of energy consumption from renewable sources by 2010. It's our hope that other policymakers in Europe will take note and develop equally supportive renewable energy policies.'

Eddie O'Connor's talents should be harnessed by the Irish government; he is a man of extraordinary talent and vision. In 2008, Airtricity was sold for €2.2 billion to Scottish & Southern Energy and Eddie O'Connor was replaced as chief executive by his former business partner Paul Downing. On his departure, Downing paid tribute to O'Connor: 'Eddie's unfaltering belief in renewables and his drive to develop the business in Ireland inspired the Airtricity team and made Airtricity the success it is today.'

On leaving Airtricity in 2008, Eddie O'Connor set up a new company, Mainstream Renewable Power. Mainstream signed a joint venture in Chile with local firm, Andes Energy, aimed at developing 400 megawatts of wind power. In 2009, Mainstream signed a €509-million deal to co-develop 400 megawatts of power in Canada over the next four years. Mainstream will control 80 per cent of the joint venture, in co-operation with Alberta Wind Energy Corporation. Mainstream also won the rights to develop 360 megawatts of wind-generated power off the coast of Scotland. At Mainstream's official launch O'Connor said that the company's ambitions were truly international, with mainland Europe, the US, South America and Australia identified as potential areas of interest. This is a good illustration of how indigenous Irish companies can very quickly become serious global players in the international renewable energy market.

Solar photovoltaic

The latest solar technology is called photovoltaics. In solar photovoltaics, sunlight is actually converted directly into electricity. This is very different technology from the conventional understanding of solar power as a passive way of heating water.

Solar thermal (ST) is one of the most cost-effective renewable energy systems. Solar thermal water heating systems collect the sun's energy in the form of heat. The system can save a major portion of your utility bill, as you will not need as much gas or electricity to heat water for your home: the sun will do most of the work. Sunlight (always free) heats your water from a regular temperature to a temperature somewhere between 50–70 °F/10–21 °C). This drastically reduces water heating costs.

But photovoltaic, now the biggest generator of solar energy around the world, works as follows: sunlight is made of photons, small particles of energy. These photons are absorbed by and pass through the material (silicon) of a solar cell or solar photovoltaic panel. The photons 'agitate' the electrons found in the material of the photovoltaic cell. As they begin to move (or are dislodged), these are 'routed' into a current. This, technically, is electricity – the movement of electrons along a path. Wire conducts these electrons either to batteries or to the regular electrical system of a house, to be used by appliances and other household electrical items. In many solar energy systems, the battery stores energy for later use.

World solar photovoltaic (PV) market installations reached a record high of 5.95 gigawatts (GW) in 2008, representing growth of 110 per cent over the previous year.

Europe accounted for 82 per cent of world demand in 2008. Spain's 285 per cent growth pushed Germany into second place in the market ranking, while the US advanced to number three. Rapid growth in Korea allowed it to become the fourth largest market, closely followed by Italy and Japan. In the assessment of PV demand in 2008, eighty-one countries contributed to the 5.95 GW world market total.

On the supply side, world solar cell production reached a consolidated figure of 6.85 GW in 2008, up from 3.44 GW a year earlier. Overall capacity utilisation rose to 67 per cent in 2008 from 64 per cent a year earlier.

Meanwhile, thin-film production also recorded solid growth, up 123 per cent in 2008 to reach 0.89 GW (thin-film solar cells are attractive because they can produce electricity cheaper than conventional silicon solar cells). China and Taiwan continued to increase their share of global solar cell production, rising to 44 per cent in 2008 from 35 per cent in 2007.

The PV industry generated $37.1 billion in global revenues in 2008, while successfully raising over $12.5 billion in equity and debt, up 11 per cent on the prior year. This is going to be a huge industry. It s a technology with huge potential and, with research breakthroughs, costs will fall quickly.

In March 2009, the manufacturing costs of thin-film photovoltaic panels had for the first time broken below a golden benchmark, $1 per watt. First Solar, based in Tempe, Arizona, has brought the costs down to $0.98 per watt. The company says that further cost reductions will be achieved as technological and manufacturing process potentials are reached.

An American photovoltaic company, Lumeta, Inc. California, has developed a residential Solar S roof tile which simulates the shape of clay and concrete profiled tiles, directly replacing traditional roof tiles to become a part of the roof structure. Designed to break through the adoption barriers of residential solar, the Solar S Tile avoids making roof penetrations upon installation and is manufactured in the most popular roofing tile colours, resulting in a highly operational, aesthetically pleasing roof that generates clean electricity for free.

Biomass

Plants convert sunlight into plant matter (biomass), which is stored energy. This energy can be released with a number of technologies. Biomass can be sourced from a range of materials.

The energy removed from biomass sources can be in the form of heat, electricity or transport fuels. A number of technologies can be utilised to capture this energy.

Anaerobic Digestion – This is a process where organic material is placed in a sealed tank, excluding air (anaerobic). Bacteria then break down the material resulting in the release of methane gas, which is flammable. Anaerobic Digestion is growing dramatically throughout the EU.

Combustion – This is a well-developed technology which is fuelled by wood and other biomass sources.

Gasification – This is still a developing technology. It differs from combustion in that, when dealing with wood in particular, a gas is produced from the fuel by controlling the air intake, the temperature and pressure within the gasification chamber. This gas can then be utilised in a turbine linked to a generator, to produce heat and electricity. Gasification has particular opportunities when seeking to develop small scale Combined Heat and Power (CHP) projects.

Biofuels

Liquid transportation fuels include bio-diesel and ethanol. These can be derived from a range of biomass sources, including sugar cane, rape seed (canola), soybean oil or cellulose.

We have all heard the controversies surrounding the growing of crops for energy. While biofuels only account for one per cent of global agricultural land at present, it is already causing problems worldwide. There is evidence available that the Amazon rainforest is being destroyed to make way for palm oil plantations for use as biofuel. There have been riots in Asian countries, which have seen the price of rice increase 200 per cent and they blame the biofuel industry for using up scarce land.

This is not an industry without problems. But where there are problems there are opportunities. It is indisputable that using land to grow energy crops has an impact on food supplies and deforestation, and as such biofuel scientists say the answer is that we need to focus on improving agricultural and forestry practices, adding that average yields for many crops are just a fifth of record yields, suggesting enormous room for improvement. Their research shows that while record yields of corn top 19 tonnes per hectare, global average yields stand at just 4.5 tonnes.

The scientists argue 'It's not biofuels, it's agriculture itself that has a big problem,' adding that enhancing crop yields would prove the most cost-effective means of enhancing biofuel's environmental benefits and limiting its impact on food supplies. 'If you double the yield, you halve the area of land you need,' they say. Other commentators say that increasing use of fertilisers and pesticides to achieve these higher yields is unsustainable.

There is a lot of energy used in the production of ethanol, leading some people to believe that the end result is not as beneficial as many make out. To produce ethanol from crops, you first need to plough the ground, then broadcast seed and fertiliser; next you must spray the crop during growth; and finally you must harvest, process and distil the crop.

Ethanol from sugar beets in France comes in at 1.9 energy units for each unit of invested energy, or so they claim. The energy content of ethanol is about 67 per cent that of gasoline. The energy content of bio-diesel is about 90 per cent that of petroleum diesel.

For net energy yield, ethanol from sugarcane in Brazil is in a class all by itself, yielding over 8 units of energy for each unit invested in cane production and ethanol distillation.

Once the sugary syrup is removed from the cane, the fibrous remainder, bagasse, is burned to provide the heat needed for distillation, eliminating the need for an additional external energy source. This helps explain why Brazil can produce cane-based ethanol for 60 c per gallon.

Among the three principal feedstocks now used for ethanol production, US corn-based ethanol, which relies largely on natural gas for distillation energy, comes in a distant third in net energy efficiency, yielding only 1.5 units of energy for each energy unit used.

Ethanol and Bio-diesel Yield

Fuel Crop	Yield (gallons per acre)	Fuel Crop	Yield (gallonsper acre)
Ethanol		**Bio-diesel**	
Sugar beet (France)	714	Oil palm	508
Sugarcane (Brazil)	662	Coconut	230
Cassava (Nigeria)	410	Rapeseed	102
Sweet Sorghum (India)	374	Peanut	90
Corn (US)	354	Sunflower	82
Wheat (France)	277	Soybean	56

Note: These are conservative estimates – crop yields vary widely (Earth Policy Institute, *Plan B 2.0*).

Oil from algae

Algae yield is not included in the yield tables. To date, there is talk of yields of between 50,000 to 100,000 gallons of oil per acre. But so far, bio-diesel from algae is mainly produced in laboratory samples. Algae could lead to a 100 per cent decoupling of food and bio-energy and revolutionise the industry.

'Algae' is the term used to refer to a diverse group of aquatic, estuarine and marine plant-like organisms that are capable of photosynthesis and evolve oxygen. These organisms range in size from microscopic to many metres in length.

Algae are primary producers and provide the basis of energy and fixed carbon in almost every ecosystem in which they are present.

Since algae are autotrophic organisms, meaning they utilise CO_2 as a carbon source, they remove more CO_2 (an important greenhouse gas) from the atmosphere than they release. One tonne of algae will sequester about 1.5 tonnes of CO_2.

The amount of algae that can be grown on an acre of land is limited by the amount of energy that area receives from the sun. Algal growth estimates range from 100 to 200 tonnes per acre per year. These estimates, however, are under optimal conditions and should be considered a theoretical maximum and unlikely to be achieved. More realistic values are 50 tonnes per acre per year.

Algae can be utilised to remove excess nutrients, such as nitrogen and phosphorous from agriculture run-off (cattle, pigs, excess fertiliser) since the algae require these elements for growth. Algae can also take up other contaminants, such as selenium and some heavy metals, helping to concentrate them for easier removal.

It is possible to grow certain types of algae in the dark. However, to do this, you need to supply the algae with a carbon and energy source. Most often it is in the form of sugar. Think of it this way: for each gramme of algal biomass you produce, you need to add at least 1 gramme of sugar. It will actually be more since some of the sugar will be used for energy and given off as heat. So you will always have the cost of sugar, along with other nutrients. From an ecosystem perspective, this is very inefficient, since you are relying on some other plant to fix carbon and then transporting it to your system. It is unlikely that the financial or ecological economics of this type of system will ever balance.

The main benefits of utilising algae as a biofuel feedstock are:

- Algae do not compete with food crops;
- Algae can be grown on suboptimal land, such as deserts or near industrialised areas;
- Algae produce orders of magnitude more oil per acre than any terrestrial crop;
- Algae utilise less water than terrestrial crops;
- Algae can grow in fresh water, brackish water, salt water and even polluted water;
- Algae will not drain the earth's potable water supply;
- Algae can help remediate polluted water from agricultural run-off and sewage plants;
- Algae can help reduce global warming by sequestering atmospheric CO_2.

Depending on the lipid content of the algae, 1 tonne of algae can produce about 100 gallons of oil. Lipids are organic compounds composed mostly of fatty acids and play an important role in biological structures. They are the main structural component of membranes. Lipids are classified as fats if they are solid, or as oils if they are liquid, at room temperature.

To the end user there is no difference between petroleum diesel and bio-diesel in terms of its use as a fuel. An engine that burns diesel can burn bio-diesel. From an environmental perspective, however, the two fuels are vastly different. Bio-diesel produces:

- 67 per cent fewer unburned hydrocarbons than petroleum diesel
- 48 per cent less CO than petroleum diesel
- 47 per cent less particulate matter than petroleum diesel
- 80 per cent less PAH (Polycyclic Aromatic Hydrocarbons) than petroleum diesel
- 50 per cent less O_3 than petroleum diesel
- 90 per cent less nPAH (nitrated PAH's) than petroleum diesel
- 100 per cent fewer sulphates than petroleum diesel

In fairness to petroleum diesel, bio-diesel does produce 10 per cent more nitrogen oxide compounds (one of the main ingredients involved in the formation of ground-level ozone) than petroleum diesel. This, however, can be reduced by adjusting the engine timing.

Algae, depending on the species, will grow in fresh or salt water. It is very important to note that freshwater algae do not need to be grown in potable water. This is a very important point because growing algae for fuel will not put added strain on the world's potable water supply.

Besides lipids and carbohydrates for the production of biofuels, many species of algae can be grown to produce nutraceuticals, food supplements, fish and cattle feed, and pharmaceuticals.

There is much debate and interest in the scientific community on the direct and indirect impacts of biofuels produced from terrestrial crops with regard to land clearing, competition with food, increased use of fertilisers, high water demand, etc. None of these issues are currently associated with the production of algae for biofuels. A significant portion of algal biomass is made of carbohydrates, which can be fermented into ethanol. It is possible to derive both lipids for oil and carbohydrates for ethanol from the same batch of algal biomass.

Algae are extraordinarily adaptable. They can grow almost anywhere, including land utterly unsuited for agriculture. Since they do not have to compete against food crops for land, they avoid the problems this can cause: spiralling grain prices, food shortages, and conversion of tropical forests and wildlife habitat to plantations and cropland. These single-celled wonders also have other notable virtues:

- Algae are stunningly productive – the fastest growing plants on Earth. They can double in mass in just a few hours, allowing daily harvest.
- Algae are oily and compact, producing thirty times more oil per acre than sunflowers or rapeseed.
- Algae do not require fresh water and can thrive in water that is boiling, salty, frozen, or contaminated – even in sewage.
- Algae can eat pollution. They neutralise acids, split the nitrogen oxides that cause smog into harmless nitrogen and oxygen, and convert carbon dioxide (global-warming pollution) into oxygen and biomass.
- When algae are harvested, their lipids can be turned into bio-diesel (main product), starches into ethanol, and proteins into animal feed.

In algae, you are looking at the origins of life, organisms that have survived for 3.5 billion years and created the conditions for other life to emerge. They are the root of the food chain. Single-celled algae can crack water with a photon into hydrogen and oxygen, and then metabolise that hydrogen with carbon dioxide to sugar.

Three ways to grow algae for biofuel:

- Photosynthetically in open ponds (lowest cost, lowest control). Open ponds are cheap, but must contend with invasive species.
- Photosynthetically in closed bioreactors (higher cost, more control). Algae 'bioreactors' are enclosed containers exposed to sunlight. Closed bioreactors prevent contamination by unwanted species and reduce water use. But they cost more than open ponds because of the need for 'photo modulation' – exposing the algae to just the right amount of light. Bioreactor systems have another important advantage: they can capture and reuse waste CO_2 from other industrial processes. Sceptics note that when the algae are burned, they release the captured carbon into the atmosphere. But because algal fuel displaces petroleum fuel, net carbon emissions are significantly reduced.
- In the dark through fermentation (highest cost, highest control). When algae are grown photosynthetically, they manufacture their own sugar from water, air, and light. A company in San Francisco called Solazyme use this method. They turn off photosynthesis by growing the algae in complete darkness and feeding them sugar. Feeding sugar makes the algae produce more oil, and the

energy-dense food allows the algae to be grown in much higher concentrations, reducing costs and easing harvest. On the downside, it puts the process back in competition with food crops, undercutting one of algal fuel's unique strengths.

Future developments in algae bio-diesel could revolutionise the non-fossil fuel market.

For those of you who have been to Disneyland, Florida, you may be interested to know that since January 2009 all their trains run on B98 bio-diesel blends (98 per cent bio-diesel), manufactured locally using waste cooking oils from the park restaurants.

In Ireland, EcoOla announced in 2008 that it will invest $36 million to create a bio-diesel production plant in Thurles, County Tipperary. Production capacity and completion dates were not disclosed. The expansion follows on from the success of the company's initial production facility in County Cork. EcoOla is one of only a few companies in Ireland licensed by the Department of Communications, Marine and Natural Resources to produce and sell biofuel. Its customers include Galway and Cork city councils, Mayo, Cavan and North Tipperary county councils, the ESB and An Post.

EcoOla was formed by an amalgamation of entrepreneurs and farmers, with close links to academia and environmentalism. The seeds of this venture were sown following a field trip to Germany in 2002 when members of the group came across the idea of producing a vehicle propellant – bio-diesel – from vegetable oil.

This is the way ahead for Irish entrepreneurs: seek out world leaders in the fields that attract them and create technology transfer and joint-venture deals.

The Carbery Group supplies 660,000 gallons of whey-based ethanol to Maxol for use in the oil company's E5 and E85 blends. The whey by-product accounts for all of Ireland's ethanol supply, making Ireland the only ethanol-consuming country in Europe not importing its product from Brazil. Carbery said that it cannot increase production due to EU dairy production quotas and production caps.

Irish biofuels company AER has made a breakthrough in converting algae into biofuel which can be used in cars. John Travers, chief executive of AER, said 'There is still some additional development to be done but I guess the most important part of the puzzle has been solved in that we've proven the ability to convert it. Ireland's coastline provides prolific growth of more than five hundred species of algae, and certain microalgae can double in mass within a few days, under the right conditions.'

The transportation industry is a cornerstone of all modern economies, but it also has the fastest-rising carbon emissions of any sector. This offers enormous potential for the biofuels sector.

There are also substantial green employment opportunities in retrofitting existing public and private vehicles to reduce air pollutants. This will also require the establishment of national biofuel distribution networks.

The government needs to remove excise duty on biofuels, with immediate effect, as a means of jump-starting the industry.

Forestry

Afforestation and reforestation efforts in Ireland could play a significant role in carbon capture. Forestry management can also provide valuable seasonal jobs in economically depressed rural areas, where the only other source of employment is subsistence farming.

Geothermal

Recent advances in two areas mean that geothermal energy can play an increasing role in Ireland's energy mix: new drilling techniques allow users to tap into resources that had been too deep to access; and new ways of extracting useful power from lower-temperature geothermal fields allow productive use of resources that could not have been used economically in the past.

Power storage

Many renewable energy and emerging energy technologies are intermittent and are unable to follow the dynamic demands that will be put on them when deployed. Batteries and other energy storage technologies therefore become key enablers for any shift to these technologies. These can include such diverse technologies as hydrogen storage and flywheels that are potential replacements for batteries.

Power storage and demand reduction

Conservation and demand reduction may not strictly be part of the renewable energy and energy technology industry, but they are highly relevant to investors interested in the area. Shifts in our sources of energy over the coming ten years must be accompanied by wholesale improvement in our energy efficiency. This sector covers a range of technologies that reduce the use of energy in retail and commercial buildings, including advanced insulation, building components and intelligent systems for managing power consumption. It also includes technologies focused on reducing the use of energy in a wide variety of industrial processes.

Hydrogen

The hydrogen sector covers everything from the production and storage of hydrogen, through its distribution and the various technologies and applications in which it can be used. Hydrogen is not a renewable fuel source, it is only a carrier of energy, in the same way electricity is not a source but a carrier of power.

But if produced renewably hydrogen looks a likely candidate to replace fossil fuels in transport.

Fuel cells

Many observers believe that fuel cells will lie at the heart of any post-fossil energy architecture. Although they have been around for 150 years, their high manufacturing costs and low reliability mean that they have yet to capture any mass markets. A large number of companies and research initiatives are hoping to change that over the coming decade.

We draw a distinction between the hydrogen industry and the fuel cell sector: fuel cells can burn a variety of hydrocarbon fuels, and hydrogen can be used by other systems, such as internal combustion engines. There is, however, substantial crossover between the two sectors.

Services

The rapid growth of the clean energy industry will require the development of a complete sector of service companies dedicated to serving the needs of technology and equipment suppliers, owners of renewable energy and biofuels assets, providers of industry R&D, clean energy financial services companies and venture capitalists, consultants etc.

Nuclear

Nuclear has an important role in the future low-carbon energy economy, but people differ widely in their assessment of future nuclear power developments. The sector has to overcome many challenges, particularly issues around the disposal of spent fuel.

However, nuclear power does offer a low-carbon alternative to fossil fuel generation, and could make a very serious contribution in addressing energy security concerns.

Global nuclear power generation capacity is forecast to double from 370 GW in 2009 to nearly 700 GW by 2030. Nuclear power generation expansion will be led by the rapidly developing Asian markets like Japan and Korea, as well as the emerging markets of China and India. The market of Western and Eastern Europe, including Russia and the former Soviet Republics, is forecast to grow by 75 per cent through to 2030 and America is expected to add 30 GW. There is a total worldwide forecast investment of $950 billion in nuclear power generation capacity to 2030.

Worldwide revenues for solar photovoltaics, wind power, and biofuels expanded from $75.8 billion in 2007 to $115.9 billion in 2008. For the first time, one sector alone, wind, had revenues exceeding $50 billion.

New global investments in energy technologies – including venture capital, project finance, public markets, and research and development – expanded by 4.7 per cent from $148.4 billion in 2007 to $155.4 billion in 2008 and is on track to grow to $325 billion by 2018.

New Green Energy technology is truly a market of immense proportions, diversity and opportunities.

If we all did the things we are capable of,
we would astound ourselves.

Thomas Edison

Chapter 22

NUCLEAR POWER – WHY NOT?

A s Ireland seeks to decarbonise its fuel supply, it should look again at nuclear power.

There are many pros and cons in relation to nuclear energy, but the fact that it is 'carbon neutral' means that we should investigate if it has a role in Ireland's future energy needs.

So let us have a look at some of the arguments surrounding this debate.

Nuclear energy does not contribute to global warming and it would also give us control of our electricity supply. Many knowledgeable commentators believe nuclear power is the only real solution that has the capacity for sufficient electricity generation, which can replace the burning of fossil fuels.

Wind, biomass, wave, solar, biofuels etc, will all help to reduce carbon, but simply do not have the capacity to replace oil. Ninety per cent of Ireland's energy requirements are imported; and we are heavily dependent on fossil fuels for electricity generation.

Those on the anti-nuclear side say three of the main arguments they have against nuclear power are the accident at Chernobyl in 1986, the Three Mile Island, Pennsylvania emergency in 1979 and the disposal of waste.

As a result of unauthorised experiments being conducted at Chernobyl, one of the four reactors rapidly overheated and its water coolant 'flashed' into steam. ('Flashed' means a sudden, temporary, radical increase in radioactivity within a substance.)

The hydrogen formed from the steam reacted with other elements within the plant, causing two major explosions and a fire. The Chernobyl Russian RBMK reactor design did not have secondary containment or indeed any kind of containment vessel (unlike in Western plants), radioactive particles escaped and were carried by wind across the countryside with devastating consequences.

Equipment malfunctions, design-related problems and worker errors led to the Three Mile Island emergency. A pilot-operated relief valve in the primary system that was stuck open allowed large amounts of reactor coolant to escape. Because adequate cooling was not available, the nuclear fuel overheated to the point at which the zirconium cladding (the long metal tubes which hold the nuclear fuel pellets) ruptured and the fuel pellets began to melt. Eventually, the reactor was brought under control and there was no release of radiation, nor were there any deaths or injuries to plant workers or members of the nearby community.

NUCLEAR POWER – WHY NOT?

Three Mile Island brought about immediate sweeping changes in the US nuclear industry, involving emergency response planning, reactor operator training, human factors engineering, radiation protection, and many other areas of nuclear power plant operations. It also caused the US Nuclear Regulatory Commission to tighten and heighten its regulatory oversight of the industry.

Nuclear technology and safety standards have moved on a lot in a quarter of a century.

The other concern the anti-nuclear lobby have relates to nuclear fuel waste. Radioactive waste has been stored in the UK without any loss of life since the 1950s. Nuclear waste must be shielded and cooled, neither of which is difficult or complex. Storage in shielded concrete structures is simple and safe.

Apart from renewables, nuclear power is the only energy-producing industry which takes full responsibility for all its wastes and fully costs this into the product.

In March 2007, The Irish Congress of Trade Unions called for a national debate on nuclear power as a way of providing enough energy for Ireland's growing population.

Speaking at the launch of a Congress policy document on sustainable energy, General Secretary David Begg said that he was not 'cheerleading' for nuclear power. However, he said that within five years it must be acknowledged that some energy imported from the UK would undoubtedly be generated by nuclear means. He accused the government of a lack of 'joined-up thinking' in its formulation of energy policy.

Congress also called for the establishment of a National Energy Agency. It said the energy issue is too serious to be left in the hands of politicians engaging in 'electoral gimmickry'.

In April 2006, the state agency, Forfás, informed the government that Ireland will face a liquid fuel crisis in the next ten to fifteen years and may have to develop a nuclear power station to supply our electricity needs. It said that Ireland is now more heavily dependent on imported oil for our energy requirements than almost every other European country.

The Forfás report had some other important findings:

- Ireland is now using 50 per cent more oil per person than in 1990.
- Irish oil consumption is 50 per cent above EU average.
- Despite Ireland having considerably fewer cars per capita than the EU average we still consume 50 per cent more oil per capita for transportation than the European average.
- Ireland is also very heavily dependent on road haulage for goods. The amount of goods transported by road doubled here in the seven years between 1995 and 2002 while goods transported by rail fell by 28 per cent.

Ireland is the seventh most oil-dependent economy in the world, and the third most dependent in the EU, after Portugal and Greece. Oil makes up 60 per cent of Ireland's energy use, compared to an EU average of just 43 per cent.

NUCLEAR POWER – WHY NOT?

'Wells to supply half the oil and gas needed to meet global demand in seven years' time are not in production today. $100 billion will have to be invested each year to develop them but it is getting harder and harder to find somewhere to drill.'

Harry J. Longwell, executive vice president of Exxon-Mobil Corporation (2002).

Sweden voted to phase out its own nuclear industry twenty-five years ago but, hampered by the lack of a cost-effective alternative, is now Europe's third largest consumer of nuclear-generated energy.

There is another benefit from nuclear power, which would be particularly useful to Ireland. Scientists are currently working on technology that will allow hydrogen to be made in large amounts directly from nuclear energy by thermo-chemical means and stored on a large scale. This hydrogen could then be used as a transport fuel.

As of 2008, France produced 87.5 per cent of its electricity from fifty-nine nuclear power plants. France is the world's largest net exporter of electric power; exporting 18 per cent of its total production (about 100 TWh [total watt hours]) to Italy, the Netherlands, Britain and Germany, and its electricity cost is among the lowest in Europe. France's decision to launch a large nuclear programme dates back to 1973 and the events in the Middle East that many refer to as the 'oil shock'. At that time most of France's electricity came from oil-burning plants. France has very few natural energy resources. It has no oil, no gas, her coal resources are very poor and virtually exhausted. French policymakers saw only one way for France to achieve energy independence: nuclear energy, a source of energy so compact that a few pounds of fissionable uranium is all the fuel needed to run a big city for a year. Plans were drawn up to introduce the most comprehensive national nuclear energy programme in history. Over the next fifteen years France installed enough nuclear reactors to satisfy all its power needs.

How was France able to get its people to accept nuclear power? What is about French culture and politics that allowed them to succeed where most other countries have failed? There are three main reasons:

First, the French are an independent people. The thought of being dependent for energy on a volatile region of the world such as the Middle East disturbed many in France. Citizens quickly accepted that nuclear power might be a necessity. A popular French riposte to the question of why they have so much nuclear energy is 'no oil, no gas, no coal, no choice'.

Second, there are cultural factors. France has a tradition of large, centrally managed technological projects. They like nuclear power for the same reasons they liked high-speed trains, Concorde and Airbus.

Third, the French government has worked hard to get people to think of the benefits of nuclear energy as well as the risks. Glossy television advertising campaigns reinforce the link between nuclear power and the electricity that makes modern life possible. Nuclear plants invite people to take tours, an offer that 6 million French people to date have taken up. Today, nuclear energy is an everyday thing in France. Many French people have similar negative imagery and fears of radiation and disaster as most other people do.

The difference is that cultural, economic and political forces in France act to allay these fears. Another reason why nuclear power was acceptable to the French people was the decision taken in how to deal with the waste. They do not bury it, but stock it in a way that makes it accessible at some time in the future.

People feel much happier with the idea of a 'stocking center' than a 'nuclear graveyard'. Stocking waste and watching it involves a commitment to the future. It implies that the waste will not be forgotten. It implies that the authorities will continue to be responsible. This offers the possibility of future technology advances in dealing with the waste: although currently scientists do not know how to reduce or eliminate the toxicity, maybe in 100 years they will.

The French nuclear programme is based on American reactor technology. After experimenting with their own gas-cooled reactors in the 1960s, the French gave up and purchased American pressurised water reactors designed by Westinghouse. Sticking to just one design meant all the plants were much cheaper to build. Also, management of safety issues was much easier, the lessons from any incident at one plant could be quickly learned by managers of all the other plants and the 'benefit of experience' is much greater in a standardised system.

Most French people know that life would be much more difficult without nuclear energy. Because they need nuclear power, they are rational enough to fear it less. For these reasons France has energy supply security for decades to come, ensuring a prosperous future for its people.

Here in Ireland, we should only consider nuclear power as part of a comprehensive programme to limit the production of greenhouse gases; we should also promote renewable energy sources, and seek to replace the burning of fossil fuels in cars and trucks.

Expanding nuclear power is only one piece of the energy puzzle. But it is a piece we cannot afford to dismiss. The reason is clear: electricity demand is rising, some estimate by as much as fifty per cent over the next thirty years. This demand might even increase more with the coming of electric cars.

Without a crash programme to expand nuclear power, Ireland's new electricity needs will end up being satisfied chiefly by imported UK electricity, which itself is being nuclear generated.

Some objectors to nuclear power have long claimed that it is too expensive. The estimates from reactor-makers Westinghouse and General Electric is that a single nuclear power plant, running one reactor, will cost from €900 million to €1.2 billion. In 2007, China purchased four Westinghouse AP 1000 nuclear reactors for $8 billion (€6.1 billion). Last year, Ireland spent €6 billion on imported energy.

There are currently new reactor designs being developed, especially those cooled with gas. Such designs are considered inherently safer than today's light-water reactors and will be smaller, too, reducing costs and allowing more flexibility in deployment.

There is no doubt that we are approaching a peak in global oil production. The consequences of declining oil production are potentially very serious, especially if we are technologically unprepared.

Renewables presently provide about 8 per cent of Irish electricity needs (2 per cent hydro and 6 per cent wind). To comply with international agreements, we hope to have 15 per cent of our electricity from renewables by 2010, and 33 per cent by 2020.

In April 2006, one of the founders of Greenpeace, Patrick Moore, wrote the following article in the *Washington Post*:

> In the early 1970s when I helped found Greenpeace, I believed that nuclear energy was synonymous with nuclear holocaust, as did most of my compatriots.
>
> That's the conviction that inspired Greenpeace's first voyage up the spectacular rocky northwest coast to protest the testing of US hydrogen bombs in Alaska's Aleutian Islands. Thirty years on, my views have changed, and the rest of the environmental movement needs to update its views, too, because nuclear energy may just be the energy source that can save our planet from another possible disaster: catastrophic climate change.
>
> Look at it this way:
>
> More than 600 coal-fired electric plants in the United States produce 36 per cent of US emissions – or nearly 10 per cent of global emissions – of CO_2, the primary greenhouse gas responsible for climate change. Nuclear energy is the only large-scale, cost-effective energy source that can reduce these emissions while continuing to satisfy a growing demand for power. And

these days it can do so safely . . . And although I don't want to underestimate the very real dangers of nuclear technology in the hands of rogue states, we cannot simply ban every technology that is dangerous.

That was the all-or-nothing mentality at the height of the Cold War, when anything nuclear seemed to spell doom for humanity and the environment.

In 1979, Jane Fonda and Jack Lemmon produced a frisson of fear with their starring roles in *The China Syndrome*, a fictional evocation of nuclear disaster in which a reactor meltdown threatens a city's survival. Less than two weeks after the blockbuster film opened, a reactor core meltdown at Pennsylvania's Three Mile Island nuclear power plant sent shivers of very real anguish throughout the country.

What nobody noticed at the time, though, was that Three Mile Island was in fact a success story: the concrete containment structure did just what it was designed to do – prevent radiation from escaping into the environment. And although the reactor itself was crippled, there was no injury or death among nuclear workers or nearby residents. Three Mile Island was the only serious accident in the history of nuclear energy generation in the United States, but it was enough to scare us away from further developing the technology: there hasn't been a nuclear plant ordered up since then.

Today, there are 103 nuclear reactors quietly delivering just 20 per cent of America's electricity. Eighty per cent of the people living within 10 miles of these plants approve of them (that's not including the nuclear workers). Although I don't live near a nuclear plant, I am now squarely in their camp.

And I am not alone among seasoned environmental activists in changing my mind on this subject. British atmospheric scientist James Lovelock, father of the Gaia theory, believes that nuclear energy is the only way to avoid catastrophic climate change. Stewart Brand, founder of the 'Whole Earth Catalog,' says the environmental movement must embrace nuclear energy to wean ourselves from fossil fuels. On occasion, such opinions have been met with excommunication from the anti-nuclear priesthood: The late British Bishop Hugh Montefiore, founder and director of Friends of the Earth, was forced to resign from the group's board after he wrote a pro-nuclear article in a church newsletter.

There are signs of a new willingness to listen, though, even among the staunchest anti-nuclear campaigners.

When I attended the Kyoto climate meeting in Montreal last December, I spoke to a packed house on the question of a sustainable energy future. I argued that the only way to reduce fossil fuel emissions from electrical production is through an aggressive program of renewable energy sources (hydroelectric, geothermal heat pumps, wind, etc.) plus nuclear. The Greenpeace spokesperson was first at the mike for the question period, and I expected a tongue-lashing. Instead, he began by saying he agreed with much of what I said —

not the nuclear bit, of course, but there was a clear feeling that all options must be explored.

Here's why: wind and solar power have their place, but because they are intermittent and unpredictable they simply can't replace big baseload plants such as coal, nuclear and hydroelectric. Natural gas, a fossil fuel, is too expensive already, and its price is too volatile to risk building big baseload plants. Given that hydroelectric resources are built pretty much to capacity, nuclear is, by elimination, the only viable substitute for coal. It's that simple.

That's not to say that there aren't real problems — as well as various myths — associated with nuclear energy. Each concern deserves careful consideration:

Nuclear energy is expensive.
It is in fact one of the least expensive energy sources. In 2004, the average cost of producing nuclear energy in the United States was less than two cents per kilowatt-hour, comparable with coal and hydroelectric. Advances in technology will bring the cost down further in the future.

Nuclear plants are not safe.
Although Three Mile Island was a success story, the accident at Chernobyl, 20 years ago was not. But Chernobyl was an accident waiting to happen. This early model of Soviet reactor had no containment vessel, was an inherently bad design and its operators literally blew it up. The multi-agency U.N. Chernobyl

Forum reported last year that 56 deaths could be directly attributed to the accident, most of those from radiation or burns suffered while fighting the fire. Tragic as those deaths were, they pale in comparison to the more than 5,000 coal-mining deaths that occur worldwide every year.

No one has died of a radiation-related accident in the history of the US civilian nuclear reactor program. (And although hundreds of uranium mine workers did die from radiation exposure underground in the early years of that industry, that problem was long ago corrected.)

Nuclear waste will be dangerous for thousands of years.
Within 40 years, used fuel has less than one-thousandth of the radioactivity it had when it was removed from the reactor. And it is incorrect to call it waste, because 95 per cent of the potential energy is still contained in the used fuel after the first cycle. Now that the United States has removed the ban on recycling used fuel, it will be possible to use that energy and to greatly reduce the amount of waste that needs treatment and disposal. Last month, Japan joined France, Britain and Russia in the nuclear-fuel-recycling business. The United States will not be far behind.

Nuclear reactors are vulnerable to terrorist attack.
The six-feet-thick reinforced concrete containment vessel protects the contents from the outside as well as the inside. And even if a jumbo jet did crash into a

reactor and breach the containment, the reactor would not explode. There are many types of facilities that are far more vulnerable, including liquid natural gas plants, chemical plants and numerous political targets.

Nuclear fuel can be diverted to make nuclear weapons.
This is the most serious issue associated with nuclear energy and the most difficult to address, as the example of Iran shows. But just because nuclear technology can be put to evil purposes is not an argument to ban its use.

Over the past 20 years, one of the simplest tools – the machete – has been used to kill more than a million people in Africa, far more than were killed in the Hiroshima and Nagasaki nuclear bombings combined. What are car bombs made of? Diesel oil, fertilizer and cars. If we banned everything that can be used to kill people, we would never have harnessed fire. The only practical approach to the issue of nuclear weapons proliferation is to put it higher on the international agenda and to use diplomacy and, where necessary, force to prevent countries or terrorists from using nuclear materials for destructive ends. And new technologies such as the reprocessing system recently introduced in Japan (in which the plutonium is never separated from the uranium) can make it much more difficult for terrorists or rogue states to use civilian materials to manufacture weapons.

The 600-plus coal-fired plants emit nearly 2 billion tons of CO_2 annually – the equivalent of the exhaust from about 300 million automobiles. In addition, the Clean Air Council reports that coal plants are responsible for 64 per cent of sulfur dioxide emissions, 26 per cent of nitrous oxides and 33 per cent of mercury emissions. These pollutants are eroding the health of our environment, producing acid rain, smog, respiratory illness and mercury contamination.

Meanwhile, the 103 nuclear plants operating in the United States effectively avoid the release of 700 million tons of CO_2 emissions annually – the equivalent of the exhaust from more than 100 million automobiles. Imagine if the ratio of coal to nuclear were reversed so that only 20 per cent of our electricity was generated from coal and 60 per cent from nuclear. This would go a long way toward cleaning the air and reducing greenhouse gas emissions. Every responsible environmentalist should support a move in that direction.

As of February 2009 there was a total of 196 nuclear power plants in Europe, with an installed electric net capacity of 169,711 MWe and 14 units with 12,815 MWe were under construction in five countries.

In 1997, Ireland agreed to limit emissions of CO_2 to 60.1 million tonnes by 2012 but it is already producing around 70 million tonnes a year. If Ireland intends to address its responsibilities in relation to global warming and still satisfy its growing appetite for electricity, nuclear power should be seriously considered.

Nuclear Power Plants in Europe

Country	in operation		under construction	
	number	net capacity MWe	number	net capacity MWe
Belgium	7	5,824	–	–
Bulgaria	2	1,906	2	1.906
Czech Republic	6	3,634	–	–
Finland	4	2,696	1	1,600
France	59	63,260	1	1,600
Germany	17	20,470	–	–
Hungary	4	1,859	–	–
Lithuania	1	1,185	–	–
Netherlands	1	482	–	–
Romania	2	1,300	–	–
Russian Federation	31	21,743	8	5,809
Slovakian Republic	4	1,711	–	–
Slovenia	1	666	–	–
Spain	8	7,450	–	–
Sweden	10	8,958	–	–
Switzerland	5	3,238	–	–
Ukraine	15	13,107	2	1,900
United Kingdom	19	10,097	–	–
total	**196**	**169,711**	**14**	**12,815**

(European Nuclear Society).

List of EU countries with increasing carbon dioxide emission percentages

Ireland:	+5.7	Germany:	+1.6
Finland:	+3	UK:	+1.5
Sweden:	+2.7	Spain:	+0.8
Netherlands:	+2.4	Denmark:	+0.6
Portugal:	+2.1	Austria:	+0.2

(European Nuclear Society).

NUCLEAR POWER – WHY NOT?

Nuclear power plants emit virtually no carbon dioxide and no sulphur or mercury either.

On the issue of safety; we are living in a world whose viewpoints are still being influenced by the emergency at the Three Mile Island plant in Pennsylvania thirty years ago and the accident at the Chernobyl plant in the Ukraine, more than two decades ago. The truth is that nuclear plants are much safer now than they were in the past. Those accidents led regulators and the industry to bolster safety at nuclear plants worldwide. There are more safety features at the plants, plant personnel are better trained, and reactors have been redesigned so that accidents are far less likely to occur. Every US nuclear plant has an on-site control-room simulator where employees can hone their skills and handle simulated emergencies, and plant workers spend one week out of every six in the simulator or in the classroom. If a serious accident does occur, US plants are designed to make sure that no radiation is released into the environment. Reactors are contained inside a huge structure of reinforced concrete with walls that are as much as 4 feet thick; the Chernobyl reactor lacked such a protective structure.

Coal mining worldwide results in several thousand deaths every year and burning coal is a leading source of mercury in the atmosphere.

If you look at safety more broadly, from an environmental perspective, the death and destruction stemming from global warming will far exceed what is likely to happen in the event of a nuclear accident. Yet, when we talk about safety all we seem to focus on are the risks of nuclear power.

Ireland is faced with a high level of oil dependency at a time when plentiful oil can no longer be guaranteed and when its use is becoming increasingly questioned on environmental grounds.

I don't say that nuclear power is the only alternative, but it is one alternative and it should be considered. We should have a national debate on the matter and the sooner the better.

Chapter 23

THE BUDGET APRIL 2009

I n its April 2009 budget the government decided to follow a monetarist, contractionary policy when what was needed was an expansionary one. Much of Ireland's economic progress over the last couple of decades could now be reversed. Ireland needs to return to an export-led economy. To do that, reducing the cost base of the state is necessary. This Budget focused far too much on taxation and cuts in capital spending and not enough on reducing the public sector cost base, especially pay and pensions. Moreover, the tax increases were levied almost exclusively on labour.

There were many painful aspects to the Irish budget of April 2009 for ordinary Irish taxpayers. But the measure that will prove to be the most painful of all for the people of Ireland in the years ahead is the proposal to bail out Ireland's multimillionaire property speculators and insolvent banks by having the Irish taxpayers assume responsibility for billions of their rancid debts.

To that end, the finance minister announced the establishment of the National Asset Management Agency (NAMA) to take bad loans off the balance sheets of the major banks. The agency will form part of the National Treasury Management Agency (NTMA).

Former Swedish Finance Minister comments on Ireland's 'bad bank' plan

Former Swedish Minister for Finance Bo Lundgren, the man hailed as a hero after saving the Swedish banks in the early 1990s has warned that the Irish taxpayer is being forced to take on too much risk under the government's 'bad bank' plan. When he was interviewed on RTÉ radio on 12 April 2009 he said, 'the problem with bad assets are, if not worthless, they are worth a lot less than the nominal value and to be able to price them in a way where the taxpayer doesn't lose a lot of money in the end, it is difficult.'

Lungren noted the Swedish did not buy any toxic debts.

In an *Irish Times* article on 17 April twenty of Ireland's leading academic economists argued that the Government got it badly wrong in relation to NAMA and it was not the way to clean up the banking mess created by the property bubble.

When asked to comment on the eminent economists' view Brian Cowen dismissed it with 'that's their view', which is precisely the sort of ignorant discarding of expert advice that got Ireland into the current economic mess.

When Brian Cowen was Minister for Finance in 2004 he sowed the seeds for Ireland's current economic crisis by fuelling the property bubble instead of reining it in. He made billionaires of the speculators and bankers and in the process bankrupted the nation. Now as Taoiseach Brian Cowen is going to double the already astronomical national debt in an attempt to put even more money into these people's pockets.

In introducing this bad bank proposal, Finance Minister Brian Lenihan said, 'Our sole objective is to ensure that householders can access credit for home loans and consumer credit, that small and medium-sized business can fund their enterprises, that deposit-holders have confidence that their money is secure and protected, and that international investors are satisfied about the stability of our banking system.' If the sole objective was to free up credit for householders and consumer credit, then he should have bailed out the Irish taxpayers and not the property speculators and bankers.

The government created the bank guarantee of €485 billion for this purpose and it failed to work; they recapitalised the banks with €7 billion and it failed to work; and this new measure will also fail beacuse the Irish banks are insolvent and should be allowed to go into bankruptcy.

In Brian Lenihan's own words 'Here in Ireland, through the bank guarantee, bank recapitalisation and the protection of public ownership, we have provided very substantial support to the banking sector'. But none of that support has worked, because Irish small businesses are going broke from lack of credit and finance and our unemployment rate keeps soaring.

Over the past five years the bankers created huge amounts of magic and exotic instruments that would make *them* rich – CDOs, CDUs SIVs, etc. – and there are now massive amounts of these financial instruments floating around, billions and billions worth, which are going to come back and cause massive problems.

If the government keeps trying to bail out the banks it will eventually be forced to face reality when it finally runs out of cash, but of course at that stage it will be too late for us as all the money will have been wasted and the country will be broke and we will begin to default on our international debt. If that occurs it is 'game over'.

The government's view that the banks' toxic assets are incorrectly priced due to illiquidity is wrong. The low prices of these toxic assets actually reflect the fundamentals, rather than being driven by an illiquid market. The government is mistaking a solvency crisis for a liquidity crisis.

Many of the major Irish banks are now legitimately insolvent. This insolvency can no longer be viewed as a result of bank assets being marked to artificially depressed prices in an illiquid market.

In short, the government cannot save the banks by improving liquidity or changing valuation rules because the problem is not illiquidity or accounting. The problem is that these highly leveraged banks own assets that are worth far less than they thought they would be, and the banks are insolvent as a result. Instead of supporting these zombie banks, the government should allow them to fail and seize the good assets. But that is not on the government agenda. Under the current government proposals:

Banks win. Investors win. Taxpayers lose.

In addition to this we need to reduce the debt overhang for tens of thousands of insolvent householders throughout the country via a 50 per cent reduction of the face value of all owner-occupied residential mortgages.

When I visited Russia back in 1992–3 as part of the EU-TACIS programme (Technical Assistance for the Confederation of Independent States & Russia), our brief was to see how the EU could assist in the privatisation of Russian agriculture. Prior to the fall of communism the Russian agricultural sector was dominated by very large (200,000-hectare), state-owned, collective farms. Like much of the communist system, agricultural production had collapsed and the EU was concerned that this should be rectified as part of support for the country's fledgling democracy. But at that that time Russia had no money, because the war in Afghanistan and the arms race had bankrupted the country.

We proposed that the collective farms be broken up, giving each worker about 100 hectares, which would allow the farmers to use the land as collateral to buy new machinery, etc. In a command (or centrally planned) economy the farmers were not used to being independent so we also proposed that the Irish Agricultural Cooperative model could be used as an overall management system to help these new farmers get off the ground and make the transition from collectivisation.

The Russian politicians saw merit in this approach, with the exception of giving the farmers the ability to raise finance through the ownership of their own land. The politicians' attitude was a result of previous communist ideology whereby the state owned everything and thereby also controlled everything. We argued that the new system would not work unless the farmers had collateral with which to raise credit for farming materials such as machinery, stock, seed, fertiliser, etc. The Russian politicians wanted themselves to get the finance, which they would then distribute to the farmers. Prior investigations had shown us that such a course of action would only help restore the power of the previous communist overlords and possibly also tempt corruption. A similar situation now exists in Ireland.

As a result of the 50 per cent collapse in residential house prices, most Irish households have no equity in their properties, all the gains of the past five years have been wiped out and anybody who bought a house since 2006 is in negative equity. So the owners of these properties have no collateral with which to raise finance.

The reduction of the face value of all residential mortgages would immediately create that collateral for every household, allowing people to raise finance, which would boost consumption and in turn give the economy its first lift on the road to recovery, thereby providing some economic activity prior to getting our exports going again. If instead the money is given to the banks, we will have a situation similar to Russia. The banks will go back to their old ways of leverage and risk which will make millions for *themselves*. They will say they cannot lend to consumers because they are already burdened with too much debt and are in negative equity.

In light of the present financial crisis, I think it is appropriate to recall what US President Thomas Jefferson wrote to his Treasury Secretary Albert Gallatim in 1802:

Banking institutions are more dangerous to our liberties than standing armies. If the American people ever allow private banks to control the issue of their currency, first by inflation, then by deflation, the banks and corporations that will grow up around the banks will deprive the people of all property until their children wake up homeless on the continent their fathers conquered.

The government should never have attempted to bail out these institutions: propping up bad assets in failed banks will not work. We should put our money into creating good assets that will grow and benefit the economy of the country. Nobody else will lend these failed banks money, so why should the Irish taxpayer?

The reason nobody will lend them money is because nobody knows what their real assets or debt levels are. They have been showing international investors their balance sheets, but nobody believes them any more. We hear much talk about Sweden and how they turned around their banking crisis some years ago. One of the very first things they did was to quantify exactly what the banks' bad debts were. That has not been done in Ireland yet. It should be done, and done properly, i.e., not the banks telling the government what the debts are, but the government going in and determining that for themselves. The major accounting firms should not be hired to do this because they all have connections to the banks and therefore have conflicts of interest.

Another thing the banks have failed to do is to explain how they are spending the funds they have already received, including the funds received since September 2008 from selling commercial paper backed by the taxpayers' guarantee. Unbelievably, the government has not put in place a tracking mechanism for these and future funds. The government is handing over billions in taxpayers' money to the banks without any detailed accounting as to where this money is being spent. At the very least, the government should have a detailed monthly report on where these funds are going. Because of the banks' previous behaviour, it would be very foolish on the part of the government to be lax in this area.

As the Irish government has failed to hold any the bankers responsible, international investors assume that such behaviour is condoned and not punished in Ireland, so they go to countries where such behaviour is not tolerated. They feel safer investing their money in such countries.

Allied Irish Banks (AIB)

Group chief executive Eugene Sheehy said that between thirty and forty big names account for half the bank's €10.8 billion of outstanding residential development loans. The government seems to be taking the banker's word that his total debts are €10.8 billion. Has the Finance Minister gone through the bank's books to ensure that this is the correct level of debt that AIB holds?

AIB has said that the bank's view is that Irish zoned land would to fall to 70 per cent; unzoned land, 80 per cent; zoned land with planning permission, 70 per cent, with existing office, retail and industrial buildings halving in value. Does this mean that Brian Lenihan and Brian Cowen intend to purchase the bank's speculators' loans at 70 per cent discount, because by the bank's own admission that is what they are worth?

Say, for example, a property developer owes AIB €1 billion for 4 projects costing €250 million each and two of these projects have turned sour and are in default. AIB can now turn the two bad loans over to the Irish taxpayers by way of NAMA and then the bank and the property developer are in the clear with the two good loans.

Dr Peter Bacon

The bank bailout scheme is a plan devised by Dr Peter Bacon. From 2004 until the summer of 2008 Peter Bacon was a director of Ballymore Properties. Ballymore was involved in property projects worth billions in Britain. It was also involved in projects worth hundreds of millions in Hungary and the Czech and Slovak Republics. Ballymore Properties is controlled by Sean Mulryan and he is believed to owe Anglo Irish Bank over €1 billion.

In November 2008, the *Sunday Times* reported that Mulryan was selling off his racehorses and helicopters. Earlier, Ballymore had to abandon plans to build Europe's tallest residential building in Manchester. Ballymore has also been laying off staff in Dublin and London. Peter Bacon says there was 'no issue of a conflict of interest' between his being a director of Ballymore Properties and his role in advising the government in the setting up of the bad bank bailout scheme.

I think the Irish government should have stayed a million miles away from a deal like this, but if they were going into it they should have hired an Irish or international economist who had not even the remotest connection with the builders and property speculators of the past decade. To hire somebody who was a director of one of these property development companies was wrong, because it is simply not a credible thing to do.

Brian Lenihan warned in his budget speech that there would be 'appropriate' punishment for those executives seen to have eroded the reputation of the Irish banking sector over the past number of months. 'The actions of those who have tarnished the reputation of Ireland will be dealt with through the appropriate processes.'

It would be nice to think that politicians who have tarnished Ireland's reputation would also be also dealt with in that fashion.

Conclusion

'We must never again let despondency envelop us'

I promised my publisher that I would end this book on an upbeat note. Under the circumstances I am finding that very difficult, but here goes.

First I must make the following points:

- The people who are telling us things will be better in 2010 are wrong. These are the same people who told us things were in good shape back in 2007, they were wrong then and they are wrong now.
- There is absolutely no slow-down in the rate of people losing their jobs and consequently there is no sign of recovery.
- Many people are burdened with high levels of debt, both with mortgages and car loans, and until the government does something to relieve this debt for these people there

will be no recovery. Instead all we hear from government, week in, week out, is that they are considering bailing out failed banks and property speculators to the tune of billions of euros.

The very fact that people are even talking about recovery at this stage illustrates that they do not have a clue what is really happening. All these commentators need to start talking about *how* we are going to help the economy turn around *before* they can begin talking about *when* it is going to turn around. Spin and sound bites will not work any more: this time we need a credible, workable plan with a timetable and milestones. To do that we must start at the beginning.

There needs to be a 'day of reckoning' for those responsible for the collapse of our financial system, by way of a thorough investigation into the causes of the crisis and identification of any who were involved in criminal wrongdoing. Identifying and prosecuting the culprits is essential to restoring confidence in our political and business establishment. The rich and well-connected should not be protected from the law and those in positions of power who made 'policy mistakes' and engaged in 'irresponsible behavior' should be prevented from doing so again.

Bankers who behaved irresponsibly with people's life savings should be held responsible for the consequences of their actions. If anyone is found to have behaved criminally they must be prosecuted.

We must stop listening to the excuse which says that 'it's all a failure of regulation'.

CONCLUSION

If we find evidence of mortgage fraud, insider trading and other illegal acts, those who were involved need to be punished. If our laws are not suitable for this task we need to pass new laws speedily (i.e. the speed at which the law governing the banks guarantee was passed – a matter of days).

This will be necessary to send out the right signals about where Ireland's values lie and will also help to restore Ireland's business reputation and help prevent this situation from happening again, at least in the near term. We need to pursue vigorously those who engaged in financial wrong-doing and we must see that justice is done 'at the highest level', by both the Department of Justice and the Financial Regulator. They need to follow up every lead and investigate every suspect transaction.

We need to make it perfectly clear that those who repeatedly break the law in Ireland, no matter how privileged, will face certain and vigorous prosecution.

In America, large financial institutions are currently being investigated by the FBI and the Securities and Exchange Commission. Those in the Irish financial community who engaged in reckless behavior, need to be investigated in similar fashion (and I mean *in similar fashion*, i.e. no more outrageously expensive tribunals). We need a new independent (without any civil servants) Financial Services Investigation Unit which is adequately funded, properly staffed with experts, and which has been given proper teeth, along the lines of the Criminal Assets Bureau and task them with the investigation. The members of this new unit need to be selected by a bipartisan Dáil-appointed Financial Services

Committee. This agency's staff should have no connection to the banking/insurance/pensions community. Contrary to what people in the financial services sector would have us all believe, the workings of this industry is not rocket science. If experts are required from time to time, they should be hired from outside. The large international accounting firms should also be excluded from the investigation, as they act for many of the banking/insurance/ pensions companies and this would constitute a 'conflict of interest'. This new investigation agency should also liaise with the new American administration and learn from their experiences and investigations.

It is extremely important for us to restore confidence in our political and banking establishment, and that will require holding those responsible for what happened to account for their actions.

This is the only deterrent, in modern civilised society, to a total breakdown of the fragile rules and laws which protect us from those who believe these rules and laws do not apply to them. If we fail in this task, we will have significantly lowered the standard of what we regard as acceptable behaviour in our banking establishment.

Public Sector

Without any doubt, public sector salaries and pensions are by far the greatest burden on the Irish taxpayers at the present time. The two-tier society which has evolved between these two sectors is not a healthy development for Ireland.

All public sector workers (including all politicians) should have their salaries and pension entitlements cut by 20 per cent. This would go some way towards restoring an equitable balance with workers in the private sector.

It would also save the government about €4 billion annually and greatly reduce our borrowing requirement over the coming years. (Considering what may lie ahead, it might be prudent to exempt the Gardaí and Army from those cuts.)

There should be a complete review and overhaul of public sector 'gold-plated' pensions and the pension needs of private sector workers should be included in that overhaul. The contrast in the current pay and pensions situation, between the public and private sector, is grossly unfair and if not rectified it could lead to civil unrest in the coming hard times.

The banks

The banks must never again be allowed to regulate themselves. We need to see the abolition of a bank's right to engage in the creation of off-balance-sheet debt, mark-to-market accounting and the 'originate and distribute' banking model.

The banks should be compelled to restore the 'originate and hold' banking model, with loans staying on the bank's balance sheet, ensuring that bank management plus its Board of Directors become responsible for loan defaults, instead of being allowed to hide these debts off-balance-sheet and selling them off to somebody else.

In future, there should be strict regulation of the banks to ensure past excesses are not repeated.

Bank chairmen should be compelled to appear before a bipartisan Government Banking Committee on a monthly basis. Any bank chairman who is found to have misled this committee, through either deception or ignorance, should be immediately fired. This would compel senior bank executives to properly brief their chairmen on a monthly basis.

This committee should produce a true and accurate report of each meeting, signed by *all* members of the committee prior to the report being circulated to the Minister for Finance. The Minister should respond back to the committee, within one week, indicating that he has read and understood the contents of the report.

The Financial Regulator

The Office of Financial Regulator should be immediately reorganised and proper accountability established. These new people need to have the capacity and expertise to alert our government, in advance, about risks developing in the financial markets.

The Regulator should also be compelled to appear before a bipartisan government Financial Services Committee on a monthly basis. If the Regulator is found to have misled this committee, through either deception or ignorance, he should be immediately fired.

This committee should produce a true and accurate report of each meeting, signed by *all* members of the committee prior to the report being circulated to the Minister for Finance. The Minister should respond back to the committee, within one week, indicating that he has read and understood the contents of the report.

Politicians

Our government has now made Irish taxpayers liable for the astronomical gambling debts of reckless bankers.

While the Irish taxpayers were living within their means, utilising debt sparingly and working hard to get ahead, the bankers were paying themselves obscene millions per year and now in their hour of self-inflicted need, they think it is right that the hard-pressed Irish taxpayers should bail them out.

In addition to making Irish taxpayers responsible for €485 billion of bank liabilities, the government has poured billions into these same banks, which have been run into ground by their senior executives and boards of directors.

We must ensure that something of this magnitude is never again allowed to happen.

The Irish banks have squandered billions on risky loans to property speculators. They also financed builders and commercial developers who used immense amounts of short-term debt to overpay for development land, shopping malls, office blocks, hotels and apartment complexes. Any reasonably intelligent person could have seen that the rental income from these properties could never have covered the interest on the debt.

One particular bank chief executive sold his company headquarters in Ballsbridge to one of these speculators for hundreds of millions, a grossly inflated figure, and loaned the same speculator the bank's money to make the purchase –

and the executive who made that decision is still in place at the time of going to press. This was surely wrong and violated the executive's fiduciary duty to the bank. That bank's share price subsequently collapsed.

This will happen again if our government fails to investigate and prosecute, if necessary, those who have engaged in any wrongdoing.

Failing to prosecute will give the signal that this sort of behaviour is acceptable in Ireland. Such a reputation, both at home and internationally, will make Ireland's economic recovery infinitely more difficult.

Our governing politicians need to have the capacity to lead from the front in all these matters. They need to understand the issues and be able to come up with workable solutions to the problems. They also need the capacity to take the tough decisions required to restore our economy to health.

In its hour of need, Ireland's ship of state needs to be manned by competent people and not by the overpaid, tired, self-serving and inexperienced people who got us into this appalling mess in the first place: no more overview committees or meaningless public relations statements, the hour is late and the Irish taxpayers (and pension fund contributors) need to know exactly what happened to their investments and this can only be achieved by thorough independent investigation.

This is one of the many tasks we, the Irish people, must achieve together in the months and years ahead. Unless we discover exactly what happened and punish those who engaged in acts of wrongdoing, this will happen again.

CONCLUSION

We need to ensure that the right people are in place to restore our financial system to full health. If we fail in this endeavour, we run the very real risk of handing over control of our economy to the International Monetary Fund.

Ireland will overcome its current difficulties: the credit crunch will work its natural course – insolvent banks and financial institutions will fold, to be replaced by better, solvent banks.

In time, confidence in it will return, our economy will turn around and this will all seem like a bad dream. If more mistakes are made by our politicians like the ones made over the past ten years our period of suffering will be much longer than need be.

There is, therefore, one word we must pay very close attention to as we set about rebuilding our economy, because the decision we make in relation to this word will determine our future and that word is *leadership*.

We need vision like that of that great Irishman, Dr T. K. Whitaker, former Secretary of the Department of Finance and subsequently Governor of the Central Bank. In the early 1960s, he formulated the plan for the modernisation of the Irish economy through the incentivising of multinational companies via tax breaks and grants, to establish manufacturing operations in Ireland. He reached the very highest standards of what is required of a 'public servant' and has done Ireland very great service in his time amongst us.

In an article written for *The Irish Times*, on 8 December 2001, Dr Whitaker said:

> Adaptability to a fast rate of change is a condition of remaining a high income, full-employment country.

Continued economic wellbeing will depend on staying in the frontline of scientific progress and high added-value production. In the past, too much of our production was in competition with low-wage countries rather than with the high-income industrial nations whose ranks we have now joined. We have the potential to stay in the frontline; it is up to ourselves to realise it. We must never again let despondency envelop us. And as we continue to advance, even if less quickly or steadily, let us be kinder to those in want.